T L Bogert
1934

ON OUR WAY

ON OUR WAY

by

FRANKLIN D. ROOSEVELT

THE JOHN DAY COMPANY

New York

CONTENTS

v

Conversations with the Representatives of Foreign Nations Prior to the International Economic Conference—The "New Deal" Shows Results.

vii

FOREWORD

THIS book, without argument and without extended explanation, seeks to set forth simply the many significant events of a very busy year. It was a year of redemption and consummation—the redemption of pledges to the people of America and the consummation of the hopes of the many who looked forward to a better ordered common life. I am setting forth the milestones that mark the achievement of a new public policy.

Some people have sought to describe that policy as revolutionary: perhaps it is. It is revolutionary, however, only in the sense that the measures adopted and the purposes that they seek differ from those that were used before. If it is a revolution, it is a peaceful one, achieved without violence, without the overthrow of the purposes of established law and without the denial of just treatment to any individual or class.

Some people have called our new policy "Fascism." It is not Fascism because its inspiration springs from the mass of the people themselves rather than from a class or a group or a marching army. Moreover, it is being achieved without a change in fundamental republican method. We have kept the faith with, and in, our traditional political institutions.

Some people have called it "Communism"; it is not that either. It is not a driving regimentation founded upon the plans of a perpetuating directorate which subordinates the making of laws and the processes of the courts to the orders of the executive. Neither does it manifest itself in the total elimination of any class or in the abolition of private party.

By almost general acceptance the people have adopted the habit of calling it the New Deal; and it has been well suggested that the phrase expresses a satisfactory combination of the Square Deal and the New Freedom. The appropriateness of this suggestion is indicated by the fact that some of the achievements of the past year will be the fulfilment of the progressive ideas expounded by Theodore Roosevelt of a partnership between business and government and also of the determination of Woodrow Wilson that business should be subjected, through the power of government, to drastic legal limitations against abuses. Thus we have recognized that in some respects government sits down at a table of partnership with business; but in others, it exerts the superior authority of police power to enforce fairness and justice as they should exist among the various elements in economic life. This combination of remedies is made necessary by the fact of revolutionary changes in the conditions of modern life.

Apart from phrases and slogans, the important thing to remember is, I think, that the change in our policy is based upon a change in the attitude and the thinking of the American people—in other words, that it is based upon the growing into maturity of our democracy; that it proceeds in accordance with the underlying principles that guided the framers of our Constitution; that it is taking form with the general approval of a very large majority of the American people; and finally, that it is made with the constant assurance to the people that if at any time they wish to revert to the old methods that we have discarded, they are wholly free to bring about such a reversion by the simple means of the ballot box. An ancient Greek was everlastingly right when he said, "Creation is the victory of persuasion and not of force." The New Deal seeks that kind of victory.

The almost complete collapse of the American economic system that marked the beginning of my administration called for the tearing down of many unsound structures, the adoption of new methods and a rebuilding from the bottom up.

Three steps, all interrelated, were necessary: first, by drastic measures to eliminate special privilege in the control of the old economic and social structure by a numerically very small but very powerful group of individuals so set in authority that they dominated business and banking and government itself; second, to war on crime and graft and to build up moral values; and third, to seek a return of the swing of the pendulum, which for three generations had been sweeping toward a constantly increasing concentration of wealth in fewer and fewer hands—a swing back in the direction of a wider distribution of the wealth and property of the nation.

The time called for and still calls for planning. This book describes the nature and the purpose of the many factors that were necessary to the working out of a national plan for improvement. In spite of the necessary complexity of the group of organizations whose abbreviated titles have caused some amusement, and through what has seemed to some a mere reaching out for centralized power by the Federal Government, there has run a very definite, deep and permanent objective.

With regard to the individual excellence of each one of them, I can only repeat what I have often said—that the individual parts in this planned program are by no means inflexible or infallible. In some respects we may have to change the method; in others, we may not have gone far enough. Time and experience will teach us many things.

I do not hope in this book to argue by an accumulation of detailed information the results of all of the factors of the New Deal. A few generalizations, however, are admissible.

The value of our farm crops has greatly risen over the prices received for them during the previous year; the machinery of most of our industries is turning out a greatly increased production of goods, and these goods are being bought by the consuming public; the freight carrying and the passenger travel of our railroads and other transportation facilities have improved; the distress of mortgagors is being lightened; relief for the unemployed who were in great need has in large part carried out the purpose of the Administration that it would use every endeavor to prevent starvation; the conservation of resources, the prevention of floods and the general planning for the better use of our wide land, have proceeded at a pace undreamed of in the past.

A year ago things were going wrong with our civilization. We might as well admit it. We know at least the ideals of the men and women who settled America. We know at least the ideals of the founders of the Republic. In the latter years, conditions had greatly changed—perhaps we had not forgotten the older ideals, but at least we were disregarding most of them.

We, the people of this country, do not need, nor do we seek for criticism or for opposition that is merely destructive: such individuals or associations of individuals, which for political or selfish financial reasons oppose the broad objective, will,

we know, harm only themselves, for we as a people will never go along with any proposal that the country return to the conditions of the decade which followed the World War. An overwhelming majority of our people however, old and young, and especially the young, are ready to give honest heed to honest suggestions for new and better methods to accomplish a common purpose. In any event, we as a people are determined, after going forward for one year, to keep on going forward some more.

ON OUR WAY

CHAPTER ONE

THE first act of the Administration was the swearing in of the new Cabinet in the President's study in the White House, immediately after the close of the Inaugural Parade on March fourth. At this time no formal meeting of the Cabinet was held, but I discussed the banking situation with the Secretary of the Treasury and the Attorney General, asking them to be prepared the next day to outline a constitutional method of closing all banks.

This was made necessary by the existing situation. Practically every bank was closed either because of voluntary action, depositors' runs or Governors' proclamations. The objective was to get the banks reopened as soon as possible, but this reopening process had to be based not only upon public confidence but upon a uniform plan which would make it certain that only solvent banks would commence business again.

Nearly two months previously I had discussed with a number of people the authority of the

President to assume jurisdiction over a banking crisis by closing all banks—not only those which were members of the Federal Reserve System but also State non-member banks. A friend of mine suggested that some of the war emergency legislation of 1917 had not been repealed and found for me a statute of that year covering the point. During the month of February, Senator Walsh, who was slated to be the Attorney General in the new Cabinet, carefully explored this statute and told me that in his judgment it had not been actually repealed by a subsequent general act. On March third, after the unfortunate death of Senator Walsh, I told these facts to Mr. Homer Cummings, whom I had invited to become Attorney General, and asked him to be ready to render an opinion at a moment's notice.

The first meeting of the new Cabinet was on Sunday afternoon, March fifth. Secretary Woodin had been in almost continuous conferences with the outgoing officials of the Treasury Department for three days. They had unselfishly rendered every possible help to him. By Sunday he and I were fully convinced that the drastic action of closing the banks was necessary in order to prevent complete chaos on Monday morning. At the Cabinet meeting I turned to Attorney General Cummings and asked him for his report on the constitutionality of the proposed action. He replied that he had examined the statutes and was

4

ready to assure me of the complete validity of my proposed proclamation.

Because of its historical and constitutional implications this proclamation is printed in full.

WHEREAS there have been heavy and unwarranted withdrawals of gold and currency from our banking institutions for the purpose of hoarding; and

WHEREAS continuous and increasingly extensive speculative activity abroad in foreign exchange has resulted in severe drains on the Nation's stocks of gold; and

WHEREAS these conditions have created a national emergency; and

WHEREAS it is in the best interests of all bank depositors that a period of respite be provided with a view to preventing further hoarding of coin, bullion or currency or speculation in foreign exchange and permitting the application of appropriate measures to protect the interests of our people; and

WHEREAS it is provided in Section 5 (b) of the Act of October 6, 1917 (40 Stat. L. 411) as amended, "That the President may investigate, regulate or prohibit, under such rules and regulations as he may prescribe, by means of licenses or otherwise, any transactions in foreign exchange and the export, hoarding, melting or earmarking of gold or silver coin or bullion or currency * * *"; and

WHEREAS it is provided in Section 16 of the said Act "that whoever shall willfully violate any of the provisions of this Act or of any license, rule or regulation issued thereunder, and whoever shall willfully violate, neglect or refuse to comply with any order of the President issued in compliance with the provisions of this Act, shall, upon conviction, be fined not more than $10,000, or, if a natural person, imprisoned for not more than ten years, or both; * * *";

Now, THEREFORE, I, FRANKLIN D. ROOSEVELT, President of the United States of America, in view of such national emergency and by virtue of the authority vested in me by said Act and in order to prevent the export, hoarding or earmarking of gold or silver coin or bullion or currency, do hereby proclaim, order, direct and declare that from Monday, the sixth day of March, to Thursday, the ninth day of March, Nineteen Hundred and Thirty-three, both dates inclusive, there shall be maintained and observed by all banking institutions and all branches thereof located in the United States of America, including the territories and insular possessions, a bank holiday, and that during said period all banking transactions shall be suspended. During such holiday, excepting as hereinafter provided, no such banking institution or branch shall pay out, export, earmark or permit the withdrawal or transfer in any manner or by any device whatsoever, of any gold or silver coin or bullion or currency or take any other action

6

which might facilitate the hoarding thereof; nor shall any such banking institution or branch pay out deposits, make loans or discounts, deal in foreign exchange, transfer credits from the United States to any place abroad, or transact any other banking business whatsoever.

During such holiday, the Secretary of the Treasury, with the approval of the President and under such regulations as he may prescribe, is authorized and empowered (a) to permit any or all of such banking institutions to perform any or all of the usual banking functions, (b) to direct, require or permit the issuance of clearing house certificates or other evidences of claims against assets of banking institutions, and (c) to authorize and direct the creation in such banking institutions of special trust accounts for the receipt of new deposits which shall be subject to withdrawal on demand without any restriction or limitation and shall be kept separately in cash or on deposit in Federal Reserve Banks or invested in obligations of the United States.

As used in this order the term "banking institutions" shall include all Federal Reserve Banks, national banking associations, banks, trust companies, savings banks, building and loan associations, credit unions, or other corporations, partnerships, associations or persons, engaged in the business of receiving deposits, making loans, discounting business paper or transacting any other form of banking business.

7

IN WITNESS WHEREOF, I have hereunto set my hand and caused the seal of the United States to be affixed.

(SEAL)

Done in the City of Washington, this 6th day of March—1 A.M. in the year of our Lord One Thousand Nine Hundred and Thirty-three, and of the Independence of the United States the One Hundred and Fifty-seventh.

FRANKLIN D. ROOSEVELT.

By the President:
CORDELL HULL,
Secretary of State.

To provide a sufficient length of time for members of this Congress to reach Washington from the Pacific Coast, the date set was noon of the following Thursday, March ninth. Thus the way was prepared.[1]

At least a month before Inauguration I had invited the Governors of the forty-eight States, most of whom expected to attend the Inauguration, to meet with me at the White House on Monday, March sixth, to discuss many matters relating to

[1] Although this proclamation was actually the second one issued it was prepared and agreed to before the first proclamation, which was a summons sent out on Sunday evening for an extraordinary session of the new Congress.

co-operation between the Federal and the State Governments. I had had the privilege of knowing most of the Governors during the previous four years and I had expected to spend the whole day with them discussing our mutual problems. However, the national situation made it necessary for me to change the program, and because there was no time for preparation I went to the East Room of the White House and spoke to them extemporaneously, giving a complete picture of the banking situation, explaining our program and asking for their help and co-operation in carrying it out. Twenty-five Governors were present and twelve others sent representatives. They were good enough to pass resolutions expressing their confidence and their desire to co-operate; approving the granting of broad powers by the Congress; approving my plan for land utilization which had previously been presented to them; and endorsing the substitution of work relief for direct relief. It is worth noting that as early as March sixth the principle of the Civil Works Administration was born. It should also be noted that these endorsements were given by the Governors "without regard to our political affiliations." This is what I said:

I have been so occupied since noon on Saturday that I have not had any chance to prepare any formal remarks. I start off by saying to the Governors and their representatives that as a Governor

9

myself for the past four years I am somewhat on intimate terms with the duties of Governors and also with the rights and duties of States. The country needs co-operation between the States and the Federal Government. I think this has been well demonstrated by the events of the past forty-eight hours.

The States acted with remarkable promptitude in preventing a panic at a time when it might well have developed. The situation, however, did get to the point yesterday where some kind of uniform action seemed necessary, and as you know resulted in two things—the calling of a special session of Congress for Thursday, and secondly, a proclamation to take care of immediate emergency between now and Thursday.

I am very grateful for what the States have done in this emergency and we want, if possible, to have a general banking policy, that is to say, one covering National banks and State banks, as uniformly as possible throughout the country. At the same time we want to co-operate with all of the States in bringing about that uniformity. I have no desire to have this matter centralized down here in Washington any more than we can help.

The letter that I sent to you took up several matters:

Conflicting taxation between Federal and State Governments: every one of you has been seeking methods to find new sources of taxation. It has been natural and human to expect that the Federal Government should try to find some method of raising revenue.

A second question relates to Federal aid in unemployment relief: the Federal Government, of course, does have to keep anybody from starving, but the Federal Government should not be called upon to exercise that duty until other agencies fail. The primary duty is that of the locality, the city, county, town—if they fail and cannot raise enough to meet the needs, the next responsibility is on the States. They have to do all they can. If it is proven that they cannot do any more and the funds are still insufficient, it is the duty of the Federal Government to step in.

We come to the question of co-ordinating work. It is very difficult to know in Washington what States are doing well for unemployment relief and what States are not, and it is my thought that I can create some kind of central relief agency which will be a fact-finding body, which will co-ordinate the work of States, and act as a clearing house for the relief of the Nation. I hope to get that set up in the next two or three weeks.

The next proposition is the reorganizing and consolidation of local government to reduce the taxation cost. That is your problem and it has been my problem for the past four years.

And there is the question of mortgage foreclosures, especially on farm land and also on small homes. There again we have no national policy.

One State is doing it one way and another State is doing it another way. Some States and some localities are closing their eyes to existing laws and have stopped foreclosures. But as yet we have no national policy for all of this. I believe we can have one, and ought to have one.

LIST OF GOVERNORS AND THEIR REPRESENTATIVES ATTENDING THE WHITE HOUSE CONFERENCE MARCH 6, 1933

Governor Louis J. Brann of Maine
Governor Clyde L. Herring of Iowa
Governor John G. Winant of New Hampshire
Governor C. Ben Ross of Idaho
Governor A. G. Schmedeman of Wisconsin
Governor George White of Ohio
Governor Paul V. McNutt of Indiana
Governor H. G. Kump of West Virginia
Governor Stanley C. Wilson of Vermont
Governor Eugene Talmadge of Georgia
Governor Hill McAlister of Tennessee
Governor B. M. Miller of Alabama
Governor Gifford Pinchot of Pennsylvania
Governor Oscar K. Allen of Louisiana
Governor Sennet Conner of Mississippi
Governor W. A. Comstock of Michigan
Governor Theodore F. Green of Rhode Island
Governor C. D. Buck of Delaware
Governor I. C. Blackwood of South Carolina
Governor J. C. B. Ehringhaus of North Carolina

Governor A. Harry Moore of New Jersey
Governor Leslie A. Miller of Wyoming
Governor Ruby Laffoon of Kentucky
Governor Henry Horner of Illinois
Governor John Garland Pollard of Virginia
Governor David Sholtz of Florida

Mr. C. G. Smith, representing the Governor of Arkansas

Mrs. John E. King, representing the Governor of Texas

General O. C. Wood, representing the Governor of New Mexico

Mrs. John C. Greenway, representing the Governor of Arizona

Mr. J. B. A. Robertson, representing the Governor of Oklahoma

Mr. Cecil W. Creel, representing the Governor of Nevada

Mr. Frank T. Bell, representing the Governor of Washington

Senator Lynn J. Frazier, representing the Governor of North Dakota

Mr. John A. Lovelace, representing the Governor of Montana

Mr. John T. Barnett, representing the Governor of Colorado

Mr. John Foley, representing the Governor of Minnesota

Senator David I. Walsh, representing the Governor of Massachusetts.

The following resolution drafted by a committee composed by Governors White of Ohio, Green of Rhode Island and Buck of Delaware, was unanimously adopted by the Governors' Conference:

In this anxious hour of a national emergency in our banking and economic life a heavy responsibility rests on our President to lead us out of our difficulties. He is ready to lead if we are ready to follow. He needs the united support of all our people in carrying out his plans.

Without regard to our political affiliations we, Governors and representatives of Governors of States, met in conference in the City of Washington, March 6, 1933, hereby express our confidence and faith in our President and urge the Congress and all the people of our united country to cooperate with him in such action as he shall find necessary or desirable in restoring banking and economic stability.

The next two days prior to the meeting of the new Congress on Thursday were arduous and crowded. We were compelled to divide our time between the innumerable tasks related to taking over the routine duties of government and to meeting the extraordinary banking crisis. I had a constant series of conferences, with the new Cabinet members, with many informed and expert advisers and with members of Congress. The Secretary of the Treasury, the Attorney General and I were engaged with members of the Senate and House of Representatives in the preparation of the Emergency Banking Act. I suppose at least a dozen different drafts were edited and re-edited.

On Wednesday evening, with the assistance of the three secretaries to the President and the Secretary of the Treasury, I wrote out the message to the Congress which follows. The actual draft of the emergency banking bill was not completed until about half an hour before the extra session met.

On March third banking operations in the United States ceased. To review at this time the causes of this failure of our banking system is unnecessary. Suffice it to say that the Government has been compelled to step in for the protection of depositors and the business of the Nation.

Our first task is to reopen all sound banks. This is an essential preliminary to subsequent legislation directed against speculation with the funds of depositors and other violations of positions of trust.

In order that the first objective—the opening of banks for the resumption of business—may be accomplished, I ask of the Congress the immediate enactment of legislation giving to the executive branch of the Government control over banks for the protection of depositors; authority forthwith

15

to open such banks as have already been ascertained to be in sound condition and other such banks as rapidly as possible; and authority to reorganize and reopen such banks as may be found to require reorganization to put them on a sound basis.

I ask amendments to the Federal Reserve Act to provide for such additional currency, adequately secured, as it may become necessary to issue to meet all demands for currency and at the same time to achieve this end without increasing the unsecured indebtedness of the Government of the United States.

I cannot too strongly urge upon the Congress the clear necessity for immediate action. A continuation of the strangulation of banking facilities is unthinkable. The passage of the proposed legislation will end this condition and I trust within a short space of time will result in a resumption of business activities.

In addition, it is my belief that this legislation will not only lift immediately all unwarranted doubts and suspicions in regard to banks which are one hundred per cent sound but will also mark the beginning of a new relationship between the banks and the people of this country.

The members of the new Congress will realize, I am confident, the grave responsibility which lies upon me and upon them.

In the short space of five days it is impossible for us to formulate completed measures to prevent the recurrence of the evils of the past. This does not and should not, however, justify any delay in accomplishing this first step.

At an early moment I shall request of the Congress two other measures which I regard as of immediate urgency. With action taken thereon we can proceed to the consideration of a rounded program of national restoration.

It is unnecessary to go into all of the details of the famous law which was passed by both Houses of the Congress and signed by me that same day. It is enough to say that it ratified all actions previously taken, that it conferred definite and broad powers over the banks and the currency on the Executive, and that it made immediately possible the restoration of the entire banking system as soon as the mechanics of at least partial examination could be completed.

The previous Sunday, when the proclamation closing the banks was determined on, it had been obvious to all of us that the proper procedure would be to allow banks to open just as soon as we could obtain reasonable assurance of the solvency of each bank. I think that the Secretary of the Treasury and I realized that the obtaining of the necessary information would take at least a week. Nevertheless, the first closing order kept the banks closed for only four days. Quite frankly we believed that it was better to limit the first proclamation to four days and to extend the closing by

17

later proclamation than it would have been to close the banks for an unlimited period in the first instance. The result was the second proclamation which I issued on March ninth extending the bank holiday until further proclamation.

It is my well-considered opinion that the prompt co-operation and vigorous action by the Congress on Thursday, March 9, 1933, did more than any other one thing to assure the people of this country that they had a full-fledged government working together in their interests in the emergency.

During these first five days, the Vice President, the Cabinet, the Director of the Budget and I had been considering another vitally important factor necessary to the restoration of confidence. For three years the Federal Treasury had been going more and more deeply into the red. Broadly speaking, the tax receipts had continued to decline while the ordinary normal expenses of the Government had decreased but little, and in many cases not at all. People felt that we were drifting into bankruptcy without any specific plan either for balancing the normal budget or for providing definite relief measures outside of the regular budget.

The necessities of sound finance and a just use of public funds called for economy legislation

18

based upon simple facts. My contacts with the public and with the members of Congress showed me that they clearly understood these necessities. Therefore, on Friday, March tenth, I asked for the necessary authority to obtain drastic retrenchment in government expenditures. The enactment of this legislation, giving authority to reduce expenditures for practically all purposes, applying this to the balance of the fiscal year ending June 30, 1933, and also to the following fiscal year for which the appropriation bills had already been passed by the preceding Congress, gave to the country the knowledge that their Government would cease drifting into bankruptcy. The following message and the resulting legislation gave the necessary impetus to the restoration of business confidence.

The Nation is deeply gratified by the immediate response given yesterday by the Congress to the necessity for drastic action to restore and improve our banking system. A like necessity exists with respect to the finances of the Government itself which requires equally courageous, frank and prompt action.

For three long years the Federal Government has been on the road toward bankruptcy.

For the fiscal year 1931 the deficit was $462,-000,000.

For the fiscal year 1932 it was $2,472,000,000.

For the fiscal year 1933 it will probably exceed $1,200,000,000.

For the fiscal year 1934, based on the appropriation bills passed by the last Congress and the estimated revenues, the deficit will probably exceed $1,000,000,000 unless immediate action is taken.

Thus we shall have piled up an accumulated deficit of $5,000,000,000.

With the utmost seriousness I point out to the Congress the profound effect of this fact upon our national economy. It has contributed to the recent collapse of our banking structure. It has accentuated the stagnation of the economic life of our people. It has added to the ranks of the unemployed. Our Government's house is not in order and for many reasons no effective action has been taken to restore it to order.

Upon the unimpaired credit of the United States Government rest the safety of deposits, the security of insurance policies, the activity of industrial enterprises, the value of our agricultural products and the availability of employment. The credit of the United States Government definitely affects those fundamental human values. It, therefore, becomes our first concern to make secure the foundation. National recovery depends upon it.

Too often in recent history liberal governments have been wrecked on rocks of loose fiscal policy. We must avoid this danger.

It is too late for a leisurely approach to this problem. We must not wait to act several months hence. The emergency is accentuated by the necessity of meeting great refunding operations this spring.

We must move with a direct and resolute purpose now. The members of the Congress and I are pledged to immediate economy.

I am, therefore, assuming that you and I are in complete agreement as to the urgent necessity, and my constitutional duty is to advise you as to the methods for obtaining drastic retrenchment at this time.

I am not speaking to you in general terms. I am pointing out a definite road.

The last Congress enacted legislation relating to the reorganization and elimination of executive agencies, but the economies thus to be effected are small when viewed in the light of the great deficit for the next fiscal year. They will not meet the pressing needs of our credit situation. Provision for additional saving is essential, and therefore I am asking the Congress today for new legislation laying down broad principles for the granting of pensions and other veteran benefits, and giving to the Executive the authority to prescribe the administrative details. We are unanimous in upholding the duty of the Government to care for those who suffer in its defense and for their widows and orphans. The application, however, of this great principle to large numbers of people involves complications—so great that it is almost impossible to draw legislation with sufficient flexibility to provide substantial justice in varying situations. The proposed legislation states the principles and, limited by them, permits the Executive to draw the lines of differentiation necessary to justice.

In accord with the same purpose of substantial justice I request also the enactment of legislation relating to the salaries of civil and military employees of the Government. This would repeal the existing furlough plan, substituting therefor a general principle and authorizing the Executive to make application of this principle. The proper legislative function is to fix the amount of expenditure, the means by which it is to be raised and the general principles under which the expenditures are to be made. The details of expenditure, particularly in view of the great present emergency, can be more wisely and equitably administered through the Executive. The flexibility of the measures which I am proposing is not only practical but proceeds along the road of constitutional government.

Such economies which can be made will, it is true, affect some of our citizens; but the failure to make them will affect all of our citizens. The very stability of our Government itself is concerned and when that is concerned the benefits of some must be subordinated to the needs of all.

When a great danger threatens our basic security it is my duty to advise the Congress of the way to preserve it. In so doing I must be fair not only to the few but to the many. It is in this spirit that I appeal to you. If the Congress chooses to vest me with this responsibility it will be exercised in a spirit of justice to all, of sympathy to those who are in need and of maintaining inviolate the basic welfare of the United States.

I ask that this legislation go into effect at once without even waiting for the beginning of the next fiscal year. I give you assurance that if this is done there is reasonable prospect that within a year the income of the Government will be sufficient to cover the expenditures of the Government.

It was at first believed that some form of scrip or emergency currency would be necessary for the conduct of ordinary business during the bank holiday, but after the week went on it became clear that this would not be necessary. Furthermore, because of the excellent co-operation given us by the Federal Reserve System and by the State banking departments, the Secretary of the Treasury determined that we could allow the banks to reopen beginning on Monday, March thirteenth, through a system of licenses. This was provided for by an Executive Order on March tenth and at the same time the paying out of gold in any form was prohibited.

EXECUTIVE ORDER

[Regulations Concerning the Operation of Banks]

By virtue of the authority vested in me by Section 5 (*b*) of the Act of October 6, 1917 (40 Stat. L., 411), as amended by the Act of March 9, 1933, and by Section 4 of the said Act of March 9, 1933, and by virtue of all other authority vested in me, I hereby issue the following executive order.

The Secretary of the Treasury is authorized and empowered under such regulations as he may prescribe to permit any member bank of the Federal Reserve System and any other banking institution organized under the laws of the United States, to perform any or all of their usual banking functions, except as otherwise prohibited.

The appropriate authority having immediate supervision of banking institutions in each State or any place subject to the jurisdiction of the United States is authorized and empowered under such regulations as such authority may prescribe to permit any banking institution in such State or place, other than banking institutions covered by the foregoing paragraph, to perform any or all of their usual banking functions, except as otherwise prohibited.

All banks which are members of the Federal Reserve System, desiring to reopen for the performance of all usual and normal banking functions, except as otherwise prohibited, shall apply for a license therefor to the Secretary of the Treasury. Such application shall be filed immediately through the Federal Reserve Banks. The Federal Reserve Bank shall then transmit such applications to the Secretary of the Treasury. Licenses will be issued by the Federal Reserve Bank upon approval of the Secretary of the Treasury. The Federal Reserve Banks are hereby designated as agents of the Secretary of the Treasury for the receiving of applications and the issuance of licenses in his behalf and upon his instructions.

Until further order, no individual, partnership, association, or corporation, including any banking institution, shall export or otherwise remove or permit to be withdrawn from the United States or any place subject to the jurisdiction thereof any gold coin, gold bullion, or gold certificates, except in accordance with regulations prescribed by or under license issued by the Secretary of the Treasury.

No permission to any banking institution to perform any banking functions shall authorize such institution to pay out any gold coin, gold bullion or gold certificates except as authorized by the Secretary of the Treasury, nor to allow withdrawal of any currency for hoarding, nor to engage in any transaction in foreign exchange except such as may be undertaken for legitimate and normal business requirements, for reasonable traveling and other personal requirements, and for the fulfillment of contracts entered into prior to March 6, 1933.

Every Federal Reserve Bank is authorized and instructed to keep itself currently informed as to transactions in foreign exchange entered into or consummated within its district and shall report to the Secretary of the Treasury all transactions in foreign exchange which are prohibited.

Everything seemed to happen that week. On the night of March tenth word came of the earthquake and fire in Long Beach, California, and the wheels of the National Government moved swiftly to extend aid.

Events had moved so fast during this first week that I felt it important to use the radio to explain what had been done, and especially to give a clear picture concerning banks and banking to the average man and woman. So much mystery has been made of the banking business, so much fear existed in the minds of nearly all depositors, that in preparing this talk I tried to keep before my mind a picture of those men and women who had everything they owned in the world in the form of a money deposit in some local bank and who wondered if they would ever see their money again.

Here is what I said on Sunday evening, March twelfth:

I want to talk for a few minutes with the people of the United States about banking—with the comparatively few who understand the mechanics of banking but more particularly with the overwhelming majority who use banks for the making of deposits and the drawing of checks. I want to tell you what has been done in the last few days, why it was done, and what the next steps are going to be. I recognize that the many proclamations from State Capitols and from Washington, the legislation, the Treasury regulations, etc., couched for the most part in banking and legal terms should be explained for the benefit of the average citizen. I owe this in particular because of the fortitude and good temper with which everybody has accepted the inconvenience and hardships of the banking holiday. I know that when you understand what we in Washington have been about I shall continue to have your co-operation as fully as I have had your sympathy and help during the past week.

First of all let me state the simple fact that when you deposit money in a bank the bank does not put the money into a safe deposit vault. It invests your money in many different forms of credit— bonds, commercial paper, mortgages and many other kinds of loans. In other words, the bank puts your money to work to keep the wheels of industry and of agriculture turning around. A comparatively small part of the money you put into the bank is kept in currency—an amount which in normal times is wholly sufficient to cover the cash needs of the average citizen. In other words, the total amount of all currency in the country is only a small fraction of the total deposits in all of the banks.

What, then, happened during the last few days of February and the first few days of March? Because of undermined confidence on the part of the public, there was a general rush by a large portion of our population to turn bank deposits into currency or gold—a rush so great that the soundest banks could not get enough currency to meet the demand. The reason for this was that on the spur of the moment it was, of course, impossible to sell perfectly sound assets of a bank and convert them into cash except at panic prices far below their real value.

By the afternoon of March third, scarcely a bank in the country was open to do business. Proclamations temporarily closing them in whole or in part had been issued by the Governors in almost all the States.

It was then that I issued the proclamation providing for the nation-wide bank holiday, and this was the first step in the Government's reconstruction of our financial and economic fabric.

The second step was the legislation promptly and patriotically passed by the Congress confirming my proclamation and broadening my powers so that it became possible in view of the requirement of time to extend the holiday and lift the ban of that holiday gradually. This law also gave authority to develop a program of rehabilitation of our banking facilities. I want to tell our citizens in every part of the Nation that the national Congress—Republicans and Democrats alike—showed by this action a devotion to public welfare and a realization of the emergency and the necessity for speed that it is difficult to match in our history.

The third stage has been the series of regulations permitting the banks to continue their functions to take care of the distribution of food and household necessities and the payment of payrolls.

This bank holiday while resulting in many cases in great inconvenience is affording us the opportunity to supply the currency necessary to meet the situation. No sound bank is a dollar worse off than it was when it closed its doors last Monday. Neither is any bank which may turn out not to be in a position for immediate opening. The new law allows the twelve Federal Reserve Banks to issue additional currency on good assets and thus the banks which reopen will be able to meet every legitimate call. The new currency is being sent out by the Bureau of Engraving and Printing in large volume to every part of the country. It is sound currency because it is backed by actual, good assets.

A question you will ask is this—Why are all the

banks not to be reopened at the same time? The answer is simply: Your Government does not intend that the history of the past few years shall be repeated. We do not want and will not have another epidemic of bank failures.

As a result we start tomorrow, Monday, with the opening of banks in the twelve Federal Reserve Bank cities—those banks which on first examination by the Treasury have already been found to be all right. This will be followed on Tuesday by the resumption of all their functions by banks already found to be sound in cities where there are recognized clearing houses. That means about 250 cities of the United States.

On Wednesday and succeeding days banks in smaller places all through the country will resume business, subject, of course, to the Government's physical ability to complete its survey. It is necessary that the reopening of banks be extended over a period in order to permit the banks to make applications for necessary loans, to obtain currency needed to meet their requirements and to enable the Government to make common sense check-ups.

Let me make it clear to you that if your bank does not open the first day you are by no means justified in believing that it will not open. A bank that opens on one of the subsequent days is in exactly the same status as the bank that opens tomorrow.

I know that many people are worrying about

State banks not members of the Federal Reserve System. These banks can and will receive assistance from member banks and from the Reconstruction Finance Corporation. These State banks are following the same course as the national banks except that they get their licenses to resume business from the State authorities, and these authorities have been asked by the Secretary of the Treasury to permit their good banks to open up on the same schedule as the national banks. I am confident that the State banking departments will be as careful as the National Government in the policy relating to the opening of banks and will follow the same broad policy.

It is possible that when the banks resume a very few people who have not recovered from their fear may again begin withdrawals. Let me make it clear that the banks will take care of all needs—and it is my belief that hoarding during the past week has become an exceedingly unfashionable pastime. It needs no prophet to tell you that when the people find that they can get their money—that they can get it when they want it for all legitimate purposes—the phantom of fear will soon be laid. People will again be glad to have their money where it will be safely taken care of and where they can use it conveniently at any time. I can assure you that it is safer to keep your money in a reopened bank than under the mattress.

The success of our whole great national program depends, of course, upon the co-operation of the public—on its intelligent support and use of a reliable system.

Remember that the essential accomplishment of the new legislation is that it makes it possible for banks more readily to convert their assets into cash than was the case before. More liberal provision has been made for banks to borrow on those assets at the Reserve Banks and more liberal provision has also been made for issuing currency on the security of these good assets. This currency is not fiat currency. It is issued only on adequate security—and every good bank has an abundance of such security.

One more point before I close. There will be, of course, some banks unable to reopen without being reorganized. The new law allows the Government to assist in making these reorganizations quickly and effectively and even allows the Government to subscribe to at least a part of new capital which may be required.

I hope you can see from this elemental recital of what your Government is doing that there is nothing complex or radical in the process.

We had a bad banking situation. Some of our bankers had shown themselves either incompetent or dishonest in their handling of the people's funds. They had used the money entrusted to them in speculations and unwise loans. This was of course not true in the vast majority of our banks but it was true in enough of them to shock the people for a time into a sense of insecurity and to put them into a frame of mind where they did not differentiate, but seemed to assume that the acts of a comparative few had tainted them all. It was the Government's job to straighten out this situation and do it as quickly as possible—and the job is being performed.

I do not promise you that every bank will be reopened or that individual losses will not be suffered, but there will be no losses that possibly could be avoided; and there would have been more and greater losses had we continued to drift. I can even promise you salvation for some at least of the sorely pressed banks. We shall be engaged not merely in reopening sound banks but in the creation of sound banks through reorganization.

It has been wonderful to me to catch the note of confidence from all over the country. I can never be sufficiently grateful to the people for the loyal support they have given me in their acceptance of the judgment that has dictated our course, even though all our processes may not have seemed clear to them.

After all there is an element in the readjustment of our financial system more important than currency, more important than gold, and that is the confidence of the people. Confidence and courage are the essentials of success in carrying out our plan. You people must have faith; you must not be stampeded by rumors or guesses. Let us unite in banishing fear. We have provided the machinery to restore our financial system; it is up to you to support and make it work.

It is your problem no less than it is mine. Together we cannot fail.

I was encouraged and gratified by the response of the people of the country whose savings had been so seriously endangered. When Monday came and the banks reopened, great sums were deposited and I felt that the most critical period of the crisis had passed. The way was clear for the long, arduous task of economic rebuilding.

CHAPTER TWO

STRICTLY speaking the banking crisis lasted only one week. During the second week, from the moment that the banks, day by day, reopened their doors and long lines of depositors placed their money back on deposit, the most critical part of the banking emergency was over.

But the full meaning of that word "emergency" related to far more than banks: it covered the whole economic and therefore the whole social structure of the country. It was an emergency that went to the roots of our agriculture, our commerce and our industry; it was an emergency that had existed for a whole generation in its underlying causes and for three and one-half years in its visible effects. It could be cured only by a complete reorganization and a measured control of the economic structure. It could not be cured in a week, in a month, or a year. It called for a long series of new laws, new administrative agencies. It required separate measures affecting different subjects; but all of them component parts of a fairly definite broad plan. Most of all it called for readiness and understanding on the part of the people. We could never go back to the old order.

It is interesting to note that proposals for many of such measures were included in the Democratic National Platform of 1932. I was able, conscientiously, to give full assent to this platform and to develop its purpose in campaign speeches. A campaign, however, is apt to partake so much of the character of a debate and the discussion of individual points that the deeper and more permanent philosophy of the whole plan (where one exists) is often lost.

Such a philosophy of government, however, can and should underlie platforms and speeches. When read together the real objective becomes clear.

A month before the Inauguration, I had felt that the beginning of the broad program could well be undertaken by a special session of the Congress to be called for some time in April. This would have given the new Administration opportunity to become familiar with the administrative machinery and to perfect the proposed legislative program. The banking crisis, however, changed all this; and it soon became clear that because Congress was already in session and understood so clearly the necessities of the case, it would be best for the Congress and the President to press forward with the more fundamental proposals of the "New Deal."

The next message to the Congress—one of the shortest on record—quoted almost literally the language of the Democratic Platform. It was sent on March thirteenth. It speaks for itself:

I recommend to the Congress the passage of legislation for the immediate modification of the Volstead Act, in order to legalize the manufacture and sale of beer and other beverages of such alcoholic content as is permissible under the Constitution; and to provide through such manufacture and sale, by substantial taxes, a proper and much needed revenue for the Government.

I deem action at this time to be of the highest importance.

The unfolding of the program proceeded from this point on. One of the most technically difficult problems had been the restoration of the purchasing power of the farm population of the country. Several unsuccessful experiments had been tried. The farmers themselves were not agreed. As Governor of New York I had felt great pride in bringing the farmers of my State together on State agricultural problems. The various farm groups had worked almost unanimously in the development of a State program; and this program visualized not only the immediate problems of production and marketing, but also the long range objectives of permanent planning for land use as a whole.

There had been no national planning. An effort to purchase crop surpluses with Government money had ended in disastrous losses. Yet we were faced by the fact of these surpluses.

Under the leadership of Secretary of Agriculture Wallace, we held many conferences with the leaders of farm organizations and with the members of the Senate and House of Representatives who had given deep study to the whole subject. Thus we worked out an agricultural adjustment act which, while experimental in its nature, went to the root of over-production. The result was the following message to the Congress on March 16th. We aimed at action on two points: reduction of acreage in certain basic crops and relief from the pressure of farm mortgages and from the loss of farm homes.

To the Congress:

At the same time that you and I are joining in emergency action to bring order to our banks, and to make our regular Federal expenditures balance our income, I deem it of equal importance to take other and simultaneous steps without waiting for a later meeting of the Congress. One of these is of definite, constructive importance to our economic recovery.

It relates to agriculture and seeks to increase the purchasing power of our farmers and the consumption of articles manufactured in our industrial communities; and at the same time greatly to relieve the pressure of farm mortgages and to increase the asset value of farm loans made by our banking institutions.

Deep study and the joint counsel of many points of view have produced a measure which offers great promise of good results. I tell you frankly that it is a new and untrod path, but I tell you with equal frankness that an unprecedented condition calls for the trial of new means to rescue agriculture. If a fair administrative trial of it is made and it does not produce the hoped-for results I shall be the first to acknowledge it and advise you.

The proposed legislation is necessary now for the simple reason that the spring crops will soon be planted and if we wait for another month or six weeks the effect on the prices of this year's crops will be wholly lost.

Furthermore, by action at this time the United States will be in a better position to discuss problems affecting world crop surpluses at the proposed World Economic Conference.

It is extremely difficult to characterize each recommendation or law of the spring of 1933 by fitting it into a special pocket labeled "relief" or "finance" or "agriculture" or "industry." For instance, the farm relief measures were intended to have immediate effect in bringing actual cash into the agricultural regions and to prevent the loss of homes; but at the same time they looked toward the broader aspects of future land use, the control of national surpluses, the development of international agreements affecting world surpluses, and the creation of a definite demand for industrial goods made in the cities.

The next piece of legislation I recommended had as its immediate objective giving employment to 300,000 young men and taking them off city streets and State highways through the establishment of the Civilian Conservation Corps. At the same time we were doing two other things: we were sending the greater part of these boys' wages back to their families and we were tying this relief work in with the conservation of our forests, providing for increased and better tree crops, eliminating destructive floods and preventing soil erosion. Also, I might add, we were helping to build up character in the coming generation.

I think the following message of March twenty-first, which resulted in the establishment of the Civilian Conservation Corps camps explains not only the relief needs but also the broader planning for permanent national conservation.

It is essential to our recovery program that measures immediately be enacted aimed at unemployment relief. A direct attack in this problem suggests three types of legislation.

The first is the enrollment of workers now by the Federal Government for such public employment as can be quickly started and will not interfere with the demand for or the proper standards of normal employment.

The second is grants to States for relief work.

The third extends to a broad public works labor-creating program.

With reference to the latter I am now studying the many projects suggested and the financial questions involved. I shall make recommendations to the Congress presently.

In regard to grants to States for relief work, I advise you that the remainder of the appropriation of last year will last until May. Therefore, and because a continuance of Federal aid is still a definite necessity for many States, a further appropriation must be made before the end of this special session.

I find a clear need for some simple Federal machinery to co-ordinate and check these grants of aid. I am, therefore, asking that you establish the office of Federal Relief Administrator, whose duty it will be to scan requests for grants and to check the efficiency and wisdom of their use.

The first of these measures which I have enumerated, however, can and should be immediately enacted. I propose to create a civilian conservation corps to be used in simple work, not interfering with normal employment, and confining itself to forestry, the prevention of soil erosion, flood control and similar projects. I call your attention to the fact that this type of work is of definite, practical value, not only through the prevention of great present financial loss, but also as a means of creating future national wealth. This is brought home by the news we are receiving today of vast damage caused by floods on the Ohio and other rivers.

Control and direction of such work can be carried on by existing machinery of the departments of Labor, Agriculture, War and Interior.

I estimate that 250,000 men can be given temporary employment by early summer if you give me authority to proceed within the next two weeks.

I ask no new funds at this time. The use of unobligated funds, now appropriated for public works, will be sufficient for several months.

This enterprise is an established part of our national policy. It will conserve our precious natural resources. It will pay dividends to the present and future generations. It will make improvements in national and State domains which have been largely forgotten in the past few years of industrial development.

More important, however, than the material gains will be the moral and spiritual value of such work. The overwhelming majority of unemployed Americans, who are now walking the streets and receiving private or public relief, would infinitely prefer to work. We can take a vast army of these unemployed out into healthful surroundings. We can eliminate to some extent at least the threat that enforced idleness brings to spiritual and moral stability. It it not a panacea for all the unemployment but it is an essential step in this emergency. I ask for its adoption.

The mobilization of the C.C.C. began at once and proceeded energetically. By July first, 300,000 young men were in camp working for wages, a great part of which went to support their families at home.

CHAPTER THREE

B<small>Y THIS</small> time we had started our relief and reconstruction policies, especially in so far as they affected agriculture.

The next step was a protective measure—to guard investors against false information in the selling of securities. Throughout my life I had seen so much human misery come to honest families who had been persuaded to invest their savings in speculative securities masquerading under the name of investments and sold by high pressure methods, that I had come to believe that national legislation was a necessity. State "blue sky" laws had been effective to only a slight degree and I felt certain that the innocent public—and at least ninety-five per cent of the public is innocent when it comes to investments—was entitled to have the whole truth told them about every new issue of stocks or bonds. The platform of my party had promised it and I had made it an issue of the campaign of 1932. I said to the Congress on March twenty-ninth:

I recommend to the Congress legislation for Federal supervision of traffic in investment securities in interstate commerce.

In spite of many State statutes the public in the past has sustained severe losses through practices neither ethical nor honest on the part of many persons and corporations selling securities.

Of course, the Federal Government cannot and should not take any action which might be construed as approving or guaranteeing that newly issued securities are sound in the sense that their value will be maintained or that the properties which they represent will earn profit.

There is, however, an obligation upon us to insist that every issue of new securities to be sold in interstate commerce shall be accompanied by full publicity and information, and that no essentially important element attending the issue shall be concealed from the buying public.

This proposal adds to the ancient rule of caveat emptor, the further doctrine "let the seller also beware." It puts the burden of telling the whole truth on the seller. It should give impetus to honest dealing in securities and thereby bring back public confidence.

The purpose of the legislation I suggest is to protect the public with the least possible interference to honest business.

This is but one step in our broad purpose of protecting investors and depositors. It should be followed by legislation relating to the better supervision of the purchase and sale of all property dealt in on exchanges, and by legislation to correct unethical and unsafe practices on the part of officers and directors of banks and other corporations.

What we seek is a return to a clearer understanding of the ancient truth that those who manage banks, corporations and other agencies handling or using other people's money are trustees acting for others.

Every day that went by not only brought before me and the Cabinet and the Congress some new emergency need which cried out for action, but it gave us the opportunity to sift out the more distressful of the depression conditions and to move forward to the attack.

For a year or two before I left Albany, letters had been coming to me in increasing numbers from the owners of small homes who were about to lose those homes through foreclosure. Although the farm foreclosure situation dated as far back as 1920, the homeowners' loan problem had not been serious before the crash in 1929. Therefore the public was not as conscious of the increasing distress among the homeowners.

During the first month of the Administration, Mr. Henry Morgenthau Jr., as Chairman of the Federal Farm Board, had prepared for the consolidation of all of the many Government agencies which loaned money to farmers on their crops, on their seeds, on their chattels and on their farms. We were ready to ask for a huge fund to tide over the foreclosure of all kinds of farm debts and we were almost ready to extend this same principle to the homeowners.

Therefore, on April third, I said to the Congress:

As an integral part of the broad plan to end the forced liquidation of property, to increase purchasing power and to broaden the credit structure for the benefit of both the producing and consuming elements in our population, I ask the Congress for specific legislation relating to the mortgages and other forms of indebtedness of the farmers of the nation. That many thousands of farmers in all parts of the country are unable to meet indebtedness incurred when their crop prices had a very different money value is well known to all of you. The legislation now pending, which seeks to raise agricultural commodity prices, is a definite step to enable farm debtors to pay their indebtedness in commodity terms more closely approximating those in which the indebtedness was incurred. But that is not enough.

In addition the Federal Government should provide for the refinancing of mortgage and other indebtedness so as to accomplish a more equitable readjustment of the principal of the debt, a reduction of interest rates, which in many in-

47

stances are so unconscionably high as to be contrary to a sound public policy, and, by a temporary readjustment of amortization, to give sufficient time to farmers to restore to them the hope of ultimate free ownership of their own land. I seek an end to the threatened loss of homes and productive capacity now faced by hundreds of thousands of American farm families.

The legislation I suggest will not impose a heavy burden upon the National Treasury. It will instead provide a means by which, through existing agencies of the Government, the farm owners of the nation will be enabled to refinance themselves on reasonable terms, lighten their harassing burdens and give them a fair opportunity to return to sound conditions.

I shall presently ask for additional legislation as a part of the broad program, extending this wholesome principle to the small homeowners of the Nation, likewise faced with this threat.

So far in the general plan for the reconstruction of things, industry itself may seem to have been left out of the picture. This was far from being true. Since long before the Inauguration, many of us had been sorting and studying literally hundreds of suggestions and plans for the rehabilitation of industry. The oil production and refining industry not only stood out by itself as one primarily dependent on natural resources, but it was also, by law, a special step-child of the Interior Department. It took much courage on the part of Secretary of the Interior Ickes when he told me, about the middle of March, that he was ready to tackle a task which had baffled many others who had sought to limit production of oil to the needs of the consuming public, to obtain a fair oil price for the owners of oil wells and to prevent the users of oil and gasoline from having to pay exorbitant prices. He held a conference with representatives of the Governors of seventeen of the oil-producing States and, wonderful to relate, a plan was agreed on. In a letter to the Governors on April third I asked for their help. It was out of this early action that the oil administration was evolved, and although less than a year has since passed I think it is fair to say that substantial order has been brought out of chaos and, at the same time, a large part of the three objectives has been attained. In this letter I said:

I am sending you herewith for your consideration a report submitted to the Secretary of the Interior as the result of a three days' conference held in Washington the early part of this week on the oil situation and participated in by representatives of the Governors of seventeen of the oil-producing States. There were also present at the

49

conference representatives of the independents in the industry as well as of the major oil- and gas-producing agencies. The main report was drafted and unanimously adopted by a committee of fifteen, composed in equal parts of representatives of the Governors, of the major oil industries and of the independents. When this report was finally submitted to the full conference, it received the affirmative votes of all the representatives of the Governors and of those representatives of the oil industries voting as set forth on page four of the report. * * *

There seems to be a widespread feeling that an emergency exists in the oil industry calling for action and it is hoped that the Governors of the States affected, after consultation with each other, will take action appropriate to meet it.

The committee of fifteen . . . recommends certain action on the part of the Federal Government. I am of the opinion that the suggestion that the Congress pass legislation prohibiting the transportation in interstate and foreign commerce of any oil or the products thereof produced or manufactured in any State in violation of the laws thereof, is well considered. I am prepared to recommend such legislation to Congress as a contribution on the part of the National Government toward the solution of the difficulties in which the oil industry finds itself.

Again the Nation had to record a disaster. In memory of the officers and men of the U.S.S. *Akron,* I quote:

The loss of the *Akron* with its crew of gallant officers and men is a national disaster. I grieve with the Nation and especially with the wives and families of the men who were lost.

Ships can be replaced but the Nation can ill afford to lose such men as Rear Admiral William A. Moffett and his shipmates who died with him upholding to the end the finest traditions of the United States Navy.

It was, as I recall, at about this time that with measures for the rebuilding of the country crowding fast on each other, the relationship of these measures to the economic policies of other nations first became apparent. Informal conversations were held with the representatives of other nations and I extended invitations to many of their leading men to visit Washington prior to the holding of the International Economic Conference in London in June. It will be easier for the sake of consecutive narrative to group the story of the beginnings of our new foreign policy in a separate chapter.

By the middle of April things were taking concrete shape. The country was realizing that the many subjects covered by proclamations, by messages, and by legislation since March fourth, had behind them a clear purpose and that actually each measure dovetailed into every other measure. Industry was picking up; farmers saw some daylight ahead; the banks were resuming.

CHAPTER FOUR

I T SEEMED wise at this time to commence a project which had no parallel in our history. It is true, that beginning ten or twenty years ago, movements had started in various parts of the country to encourage city planning. People realized the tremendous waste of letting cities "grow up like Topsy" without any thinking ahead. Streets were made too narrow, or were located in the wrong places; business sections were overcrowded; suburban developments were mere real estate schemes. Gradually people began asking why should we not plan for the country districts as well as the cities. As Governor of New York, I had sponsored a State-wide planning movement which had its foundation in a study of the problem of the use to which all land should be put. With this went, of course, the purpose of using the land to the best advantage. We undertook to survey all of the thirty million acres in the State by classifying every ten-acre square.

Before I came to Washington I had decided that for many reasons the Tennessee Valley—in other words, all of the watershed of the Tennessee River and its tributaries—would provide an ideal location for a land use experiment on a regional scale embracing many States.

In January I visited Muscle Shoals with a group of officials and experts, and subsequently announced plans for a comprehensive development of the entire Tennessee Valley region. These plans as developed contemplated the creation of a public authority to direct the development of a region comprising hundreds of thousands of square miles.

This plan fitted in well with the splendid fight which Senator Norris had been making for the development of power and the manufacture of fertilizer at the Wilson Dam properties which had been erected by the Government during the World War. In enlarging the original objective so as to make it cover the whole Tennessee Valley, Senator Norris and I undertook to include a multitude of human activities and physical developments.

By contolling every river and creek and rivulet in this vast watershed, and by planning for a highly civilized use of the land by the population of the whole area, we believed that we could make a lasting contribution to American life.

It was on April tenth that I sent the following message to the Congress:

The continued idleness of a great national investment in the Tennessee Valley leads me to ask the Congress for legislation necessary to enlist this project in the service of the people.

It is clear that the Muscle Shoals development is but a small part of the potential public usefulness of the entire Tennessee River. Such use, if envisioned in its entirety, transcends mere power development: it enters the wide fields of flood control, soil erosion, afforestation, elimination from agricultural use of marginal lands, and distribution and diversification of industry. In short, this power development of war days leads logically to national planning for a complete river watershed involving many States and the future lives and welfare of millions. It touches and gives life to all forms of human concerns.

I, therefore, suggest to the Congress legislation to create a Tennessee Valley Authority—a corporation clothed with the power of government but possessed of the flexibility and initiative of a private enterprise. It should be charged with the broadest duty of planning for the proper use, conservation and development of the natural resources of the Tennessee River drainage basin and its adjoining territory for the general social and economic welfare of the nation. This Authority should also be clothed with the necessary power to carry these plans into effect. Its duty should be the rehabilitation of the Muscle Shoals development and the co-ordination of it with the wider plan.

Many hard lessons have taught us the human

waste that results from lack of planning. Here and there a few wise cities and counties have looked ahead and planned. But our nation has "just grown." It is time to extend planning to a wider field, in this instance comprehending in one great project many States directly concerned with the basin of one of our greatest rivers.

This in a true sense is a return to the spirit and vision of the pioneer. If we are successful here we can march on, step by step, in a like development of other great natural territorial units within our borders.

By this time we were ready to act for the protection of the small homeowners of the Nation, and this message went to the Congress on April thirteenth:

As a further and urgently necessary step in the program to promote economic recovery, I ask the Congress for legislation to protect small homeowners from foreclosure and to relieve them of a portion of the burden of excessive interest and principal payments incurred during the period of higher values and higher earning power.

Implicit in the legislation which I am suggesting to you is a declaration of national policy. This policy is that the broad interests of the Nation require that special safeguards should be thrown around homeownership as a guaranty of social and economic stability, and that to protect homeowners from inequitable enforced liquidation, in a time of general distress, is a proper concern of the Government.

The legislation I propose follows the general lines of the farm mortgage refinancing bill. The terms are such as to impose the least possible charge upon the National Treasury consistent with the objects sought. It provides machinery through which existing mortgage debts on small homes may be adjusted to a sound basis of values without injustice to investors at substantially lower interest rates and with provision for postponing both interest and principal payments in cases of extreme need. The resources to be made available through a bond issue to be guaranteed as to interest only by the Treasury, will, it is thought, be sufficient to meet the needs of those to whom other methods of financing are not available. At the same time the plan of settlement will provide a standard which should put an end to present uncertain and chaotic conditions that create fear and despair among both homeowners and investors.

Legislation of this character is a subject that demands our most earnest, thoughtful and prompt consideration.

CHAPTER FIVE

THE task of Secretary of the Treasury Woodin and of the Federal Reserve Board, the Reconstruction Finance Corporation, and the hard-working Treasury Department officials, was great. Every bank in the country, State and national, had been examined; the great majority had reopened. In the Treasury itself we had successfully surmounted the problem of borrowing enough money to meet necessary daily expenditures, although the Treasury was to all intents and purposes empty when we inherited it.

The earlier proclamations during the month of March had directed all persons in the possession of gold to surrender their gold to the banks. During this period we were of course still on the gold standard in the sense that gold could still be exported by our banks to meet foreign demands.

Early in April several symptoms began to give us grave worry concerning the gold reserve in banks in the United States. It was true that the total stock of gold here was adequate to meet all existing currency or credit needs. But, at the same time, recent history gave many examples of sudden and uncontrollable flights of gold caused by speculation or fear. Some Americans were, I regret to say, so alarmed about the future of their own country that they began to export their own capital. Others, I also regret to say, believed that if they could get their money into foreign currencies by exporting gold they would later be enabled to buy more dollars through an unpatriotic speculation. In Europe increasing pressure on our gold reserves was exerted by international speculators and by banks and individuals, who sold American securities, bought American exchange and demanded payment in gold. The result was a great increase in the "earmarking" of gold in New York for foreign account, and probably, for actual export. A movement such as this could amount almost immediately, we believed, to at least half a billion dollars. Any acceleration of it might well cause us to lose a billion or even two billions of our gold reserve. The fact is that during the short suspension of the gold embargo in April we lost one hundred millions in gold.

It was at this point that Secretary Woodin and I decided that the time had come to prevent the export of any more gold.

This was accomplished on April twentieth through a very important Executive Order which stated:

"Until further order, the earmarking for foreign account and the export of gold coin, gold bullion or gold certificates from the United States . . . are hereby prohibited, except that the Secretary of the Treasury . . . may issue licenses authorizing the export of gold coin and bullion (a) earmarked or held in trust for a recognized foreign government or foreign central bank or the Bank for International Settlements, (b) imported for re-export or gold in reasonable amounts for usual trade requirements of refiners importing gold-bearing materials under agreement to export gold, (c) actually required for the fulfillment of any contract entered into prior to the date of this order, by an applicant who in obedience to the Executive Order of April 5, 1933, has delivered gold coin, gold bullion or gold certificates, and (d) with the approval of the President, for transactions which he may deem necessary to promote the public interest.

Until further order, the Secretary of the Treasury is authorized . . . to investigate, regulate or prohibit . . . by means of licenses or otherwise, any transactions in foreign exchange, transfers of credit from any banking institution within the United States . . . to any foreign branch or office of such banking institution or to any foreign bank or banker, and the export or withdrawal of currency from the United States . . . by any individual, partnership, association or corporation within the United States . . ."

Thus we served notice on the country and on the world that we proposed to maintain our gold reserves intact.

Many useless volumes could be written as to whether on April twentieth the United States actually abandoned the gold standard. In one sense, we did not because the legal gold content of the dollar was unchanged and because the Government and the banks retained all gold as the basis for currency. On the other hand, gold here in the United States ceased to be a medium of exchange.

The next morning the Secretary came in to see me. I think that he and I felt very happy because we had cut the Gordian knot. His face was wreathed in smiles, but I looked at him and said: "Mr. Secretary, I have some very bad news for you. I have to announce to you the serious fact that the United States has gone off the gold standard." Mr. Woodin is a good sport. He threw up both hands, opened his eyes wide and exclaimed: "My heavens! What, again?"

That order was the turning point. Its result was felt almost immediately. American exchange weakened in terms of foreign currencies; and the price level at home went up substantially. Everyone realized at last that we were serious in our purpose of conserving our own financial resources, that we proposed to maintain our currency, and that at the same time we had determined definitely to seek an increase in all values.

In talking with people about our basic economic troubles I have often drawn for them a picture showing two columns—one representing what the United States was worth in terms of dollars and the other representing what the United States owed in terms of dollars. The figures covered all property and all debts, public, corporate and individual. In 1929, the total of the assets in terms of dollars was much larger than the total of the debts. But, by the spring of 1933, while the total of the debts was still just as great, the total of the assets had shrunk to below that of the debts.

Two courses were open: to cut down the debts through bankruptcies and foreclosures to such a point that they would be below property values; or else, to increase property values until they were greater than the debts.

Obviously, the latter course was the only legitimate method of putting the country back on its feet without destroying human values. We recognized that the ultimate goal was far off and that many steps would have to be taken to arrive at that goal. We knew that we should have to face unreasonable speculation, as we actually did later on in June and July. We knew that there would be ups and downs, but that by keeping the objective constantly in mind and by using many methods and measures, we could at least make an honest effort to reach the goal. When the United States went off the gold basis in April, 1933, we did deliberately what many other nations, including Great Britain, had been compelled to do against their will. The country understood that the dollar was just as good a dollar as it had been before, and that, in fact, we proposed to make it a more honest dollar than it had been during the three and one-half years of constant and growing deflation.

CHAPTER SIX

I T IS not an exaggeration when I say that if the economic conditions of the winter of 1932-1933 had continued, practically every railroad in the United States would have been in the hands of a receiver within a short space of time. With the assistance of the Reconstruction Finance Corporation, and with the increased volume of traffic which manifested itself by the end of April, we believed that all of the stronger railroads could survive. At the same time, we recognized the great unemployment among railroad workers and the need of reorganization and co-ordination of all railroads and of other forms of transportation. There was no time to prepare a complete and final program; nor were all the facts clear. Therefore, I asked the Congress for "stop gap" legislation. This message on May fourth explains itself:

The steam railways still constitute the main arteries of commerce in the United States. At this time, however, available traffic is not sufficient profitably to utilize existing railway facilities and the supplementary facilities provided by new forms of transportation.

Our broad problem is so to co-ordinate all agencies of transportation as to maintain adequate service. I am not yet ready to submit to the Congress a comprehensive plan for permanent legislation.

I do believe, however, that three emergency steps can and should be taken at this Special Session of the Congress.

First, I recommend the repeal of the recapture provisions of the Interstate Commerce Commission Act. The Commission has pointed out that existing provisions are unworkable and impracticable.

Second, railway holding companies should be placed definitely under the regulation and control of the Interstate Commerce Commission in like manner as the railways themselves.

Third, as a temporary emergency measure, I suggest the creation of a Federal Co-ordinator of Transportation who, working with groups of railroads, will be able to encourage, promote or require action on the part of carriers, in order to avoid duplication of service, prevent waste, and encourage financial reorganizations. Such a Co-ordinator should also, in carrying out this policy, render useful service in maintaining railroad employment at a fair wage.

The experience gained during the balance of

this year will greatly assist the Government and the carriers in preparation for a more permanent and a more comprehensive national transportation policy at the regular session of the Congress in 1934.

To an even greater extent than the railroads, industry had suffered from the deflationary effects of the depression. It was clear that to permit it to wait until natural forces were able to revive it would result in an intolerable unemployment problem. I therefore took occasion, on May fourth, at a meeting of the Chamber of Commerce of the United States, to make definite appeal to the industrial leaders of the country. This address is, in a sense, the forerunner of the N.R.A.:

Because of a national and a world situation which has taken every moment of my time during the past two months I have had to forego the privilege of discussing many matters of common interest with the members of the Chamber of Commerce of the United States. For the same reason, frankly, I have had neither time nor opportunity to prepare for you tonight any complete phase of our national problems.

I do not have to tell you that the Government of the United States in its executive and legislative branches has been seeking and obtaining action relating to our own internal economy and to initiation of a co-operative spirit among all the nations of the world. We have sought through moderate and wise measures to increase the volume of trade, to give employment to the unemployed and to effect a broad elevation of commodity prices.

I present to you three requests. During the past few weeks we have witnessed with a slight but definite upturn in most industries, a simultaneous rise in most commodity prices. Past experience indicates that when the price level begins to rise after a long period of declining commodity prices, wages which have been previously curtailed lag behind the rise in the price level.

That result has in the past imposed upon those who labor an unfair burden; has prevented their just and equitable share in the profits of industry and has limited the purchasing power of the overwhelming majority of our population.

I, therefore, ask you, who represent in all probability the majority of the employers of the Nation, to refrain from further reduction in the wages of your employees and I ask you also to increase your wage scales in conformity with and simultaneous with the rise of the level of commodity prices in so far as this lies within your power.

It is a simple fact that the average of the wage scale of the Nation has gone down during the past four years more rapidly than the cost of living. It is essential, as a matter of national justice, that the wage scale should be brought back to meet the cost of living and that this process should begin now and not later.

My second request has to do with bringing order out of chaos. During the past four years what previously had been considered to be an orderly industrial system has degenerated into one of the highest disorder. You and I acknowledge the existence of unfair methods of competition, of cut-throat prices and of general chaos. You and I agree that this condition must be rectified and that order must be restored. The attainment of that objective depends upon your willingness to co-operate with one another to this end and also your willingness to co-operate with your Government.

In almost every industry an overwhelming majority of the units of the industry are wholly willing to work together to prevent over-production, to prevent unfair wages, to eliminate improper working conditions. In the past success in attaining these objectives has been prevented by a small minority of units in many industries. I can assure you that you will have the co-operation of your Government in bringing these minorities to understand that their unfair practices are contrary to a sound public policy.

My third request is of a somewhat different nature though it has an important bearing on the other two. It is human nature to view a problem in terms of the particular existence and interest

68

of the company or the business with which one is personally associated. It is, therefore, not unnatural that the various industries of the country should apply this same point of view to themselves. And yet I call your attention to what must be clear to all of us: That each and all of you in your own units and your own industries are but an integral part of a great whole and that our national economy must be expressed in terms of the whole rather than in terms of the unit.

It is ultimately of little avail to any of you to be temporarily prosperous while others are permanently depressed. I ask that you translate your welfare into the welfare of the whole, that you view recovery in terms of the Nation rather than in terms of a particular industry, that you have the vision to lay aside special and selfish interests, to think of and act for a well-rounded national recovery.

May I take this opportunity to express my special appreciation of the fine co-operation which I have had from your President, Mr. Harriman, and from his associates. He has felt free to call on me and I have felt free to call on him. In that spirit the Nation is working itself out of its troubles. In that spirit we shall succeed.

This was followed on May seventh by a general radio address, the first since that on banks early in March. It afforded me the opportunity to review the many events of the first two months of my administration.

On a Sunday night a week after my Inauguration I used the radio to tell you about the banking crisis and the measures we were taking to meet it. I think that in that way I made clear to the country various facts that might otherwise have been misunderstood and in general provided a means of understanding which did much to restore confidence.

Tonight, eight weeks later, I come for the second time to give you my report—in the same spirit and by the same means to tell you about what we have been doing and what we are planning to do.

Two months ago we were facing serious problems. The country was dying by inches. It was dying because trade and commerce had declined to dangerously low levels; prices for basic commodities were such as to destroy the value of the assets of national institutions such as banks, savings banks, insurance companies, and others. These institutions, because of their great needs, were foreclosing mortgages, calling loans, refusing credit. Thus there was actually in process of destruction the property of millions of people who had borrowed money on that property in terms of dollars which had had an entirely different value from the level of March, 1933. That situation in that crisis did not call for any complicated consideration of economic panaceas or fancy plans. We were faced by a condition and not a theory.

There were just two alternatives: The first was to allow the foreclosures to continue, credit to be withheld and money to go into hiding, and thus forcing liquidation and bankruptcy of banks, railroads and insurance companies and a recapitalizing of all business and all property on a lower level. This alternative meant a continuation of what is loosely called "deflation," the net result of which would have been extraordinary hardship on all property owners and, incidentally, extraordinary hardship on all persons working for wages through an increase in unemployment and a further reduction of the wage scale.

It is easy to see that the result of this course would have not only economic effects of a very serious nature but social results that might bring incalculable harm. Even before I was inaugurated I came to the conclusion that such a policy was too much to ask the American people to bear. It involved not only a further loss of homes, farms, savings and wages but also a loss of spiritual values —the loss of that sense of security for the present and the future so necessary to the peace and contentment of the individual and of his family. When you destroy these things you will find it difficult to establish confidence of any sort in the future. It was clear that mere appeals from Washington for confidence and the mere lending of more money to shaky institutions could not stop this downward course. A prompt program applied as quickly as possible seemed to me not only justified but imperative to our national security. The Congress, and when I say Congress I mean the members of both political parties, fully understood this and gave me generous and intelligent support. The members of Congress realized that the methods of normal times had to be replaced in the emergency by measures which were suited to the serious and pressing requirements of the moment. There was no actual surrender of power, Congress still retained its constitutional authority and no one has the slightest desire to change the balance of these powers. The function of Congress is to decide what has to be done and to select the appropriate agency to carry out its will. This policy it has strictly adhered to. The only thing that has been happening has been to designate the President as the agency to carry out certain of the purposes of the Congress. This was constitutional and in keeping with the past American tradition.

The legislation which has been passed or in the process of enactment can properly be considered as part of a well-grounded plan.

First, we are giving opportunity of employment to one-quarter of a million of the unemployed, especially the young men who have dependents, to go into the forestry and flood prevention work. This is a big task because it means feeding, clothing and caring for nearly twice as many men as we have in the regular army itself. In creating this civilian conservation corps we are killing two birds with one stone. We are clearly enhancing the value of our natural resources and second, we are relieving an appreciable amount of actual distress. This great group of men has entered upon its work on a purely voluntary basis, no military training is involved and we are conserving not only our natural resources but our human resources. One of the great values to this work is the fact that it is direct and requires the intervention of very little machinery.

Second, I have requested the Congress and have secured action upon a proposal to put the great properties owned by our Government at Muscle Shoals to work after long years of wasteful inaction, and with this a broad plan for the improvement of a vast area in the Tennessee Valley. It will add to the comfort and happiness of hundreds of thousands of people and the incident benefits will reach the entire Nation.

Next, the Congress is about to pass legislation that will greatly ease the mortgage distress among the farmers and the homeowners of the nation, by providing for the easing of the burden of debt now bearing so heavily upon millions of our people.

Our next step in seeking immediate relief is a grant of half a billion dollars to help the States, counties and municipalities in their duty to care for those who need direct and immediate relief.

The Congress also passed legislation authorizing the sale of beer in such States as desired. This has already resulted in considerable re-employment and incidentally has provided much needed tax revenue.

We are planning to ask the Congress for legislation to enable the Government to undertake public works, thus stimulating directly and indirectly the employment of many others in well-considered projects.

Further legislation has been taken up which goes much more fundamentally into our economic problems. The Farm Relief Bill seeks by the use of several methods, alone or together, to bring about an increased return to farmers for their major farm products, seeking at the same time to prevent in the days to come disastrous over-production which so often in the past has kept farm commodity prices far below a reasonable return. This measure provides wide powers for emergencies. The extent of its use will depend entirely upon what the future has in store.

Well-considered and conservative measures will likewise be proposed which will attempt to give to the industrial workers of the country a more fair wage return, prevent cut-throat competition and unduly long hours for labor, and at the same time to encourage each industry to prevent over-production.

Our Railroad Bill falls into the same class because it seeks to provide and make certain definite planning by the railroads themselves, with the assistance of the Government, to eliminate the duplication and waste that is now resulting in railroad receiverships and continuing operating deficits.

I am certain that the people of this country understand and approve the broad purposes behind these new governmental policies relating to agriculture and industry and transportation. We found ourselves faced with more agricultural products than we could possibly consume ourselves and surpluses which other nations did not have the cash to buy from us except at prices ruinously low. We have found our factories able to turn out more goods than we could possibly consume, and at the same time we were faced with a falling export demand. We found ourselves with more facilities to transport goods and crops than there were goods and crops to be transported. All of this has been caused in large part by a complete lack of planning and a complete failure to understand the danger signals that have been flying ever since the close of the World War. The people of this country have been erroneously encouraged to believe that they could keep on increasing the output of farm and factory indefinitely and that some magician would find ways and means for that increased output to be consumed with reasonable profit to the producer.

Today we have reason to believe that things are a little better than they were two months ago.

Industry has picked up, railroads are carrying more freight, farm prices are better, but I am not going to indulge in issuing proclamations of over-enthusiastic assurance. We cannot bally-hoo ourselves back to prosperity. I am going to be honest at all times with the people of the country. I do not want the people of this country to take the foolish course of letting this improvement come back on another speculative wave. I do not want the people to believe that because of unjustified optimism we can resume the ruinous practice of increasing our crop output and our factory output in the hope that a kind Providence will find buyers at high prices. Such a course may bring us immediate and false prosperity but it will be the kind of prosperity that will lead us into another tailspin.

It is wholly wrong to call the measures that we have taken government control of farming, control of industry, and control of transportation. It is rather a partnership between Government and farming and industry and transportation, not partnership in profits, for the profits would still go to the citizens, but rather a partnership in planning and partnership to see that the plans are carried out.

Let me illustrate with an example. Take the cotton goods industry. It is probably true that ninety per cent of the cotton manufacturers would agree to eliminate starvation wages, would agree to stop long hours of employment, would agree to stop child labor, would agree to prevent an over-production that would result in unsalable surpluses. But, what good is such an agreement if the other ten per cent of cotton manufacturers pay starvation wages, require long hours, employ children in their mills and turn out burdensome surpluses? The unfair ten per cent could produce goods so cheaply that the fair ninety per cent would be compelled to meet the unfair conditions. Here is where government comes in. Government ought to have the right and will have the right, after surveying and planning for an industry to prevent, with the assistance of the overwhelming majority of that industry, unfair practice and to enforce this agreement by the authority of government. The so-called anti-trust laws were intended to prevent the creation of monopolies and to forbid unreasonable profits to those monopolies. That purpose of the anti-trust laws must be continued, but these laws were never intended to encourage the kind of unfair competition that results in long hours, starvation wages and over-production.

The same principle applies to farm products and to transportation and every other field of organized private industry.

We are working toward a definite goal, which is to prevent the return of conditions which came very close to destroying what we call modern civilization. The actual accomplishment of our purpose cannot be attained in a day. Our policies are wholly within purposes for which our American Constitutional Government was established 150 years ago.

I know that the people of this country will understand this and will also understand the spirit in which we are undertaking this policy. I do not deny that we may make mistakes of procedure as we carry out the policy. I have no expectation of making a hit every time I come to bat. What I seek is the highest possible batting average, not only for myself but for the team. Theodore Roosevelt once said to me: "If I can be right 75 per cent of the time I shall come up to the fullest measure of my hopes."

Much has been said of late about Federal finances and inflation, the gold standard, etc. Let me make the facts very simple and my policy very clear. In the first place, government credit and government currency are really one and the same thing. Behind government bonds there is only a promise to pay. Behind government currency we have, in addition to the promise to pay, a reserve of gold and a small reserve of silver. In this connection it is worth while remembering that in the past the Government has agreed to redeem nearly thirty billions of its debts and its currency in gold, and private corporations in this country have agreed to redeem another sixty or seventy billions of securities and mortgages in gold. The Government and private corporations were making these agreements when they knew full well that all of the gold in the United States amounted to only between three and four billions and that all of the gold in all of the world amounted to only about eleven billions.

If the holders of these promises to pay started in to demand gold the first comers would get gold for a few days and they would amount to about one twenty-fifth of the holders of the securities and the currency. The other twenty-four people out of twenty-five, who did not happen to be at the top of the line, would be told politely that there was no more gold left. We have decided to treat all twenty-five in the same way in the interests of justice and the exercise of the constitutional powers of this Government. We have placed everyone on the same basis in order that the general good may be preserved.

Nevertheless, gold, and to a partial extent silver, are perfectly good bases for currency and that is why I decided not to let any of the gold now in the country go out of it.

A series of conditions arose three weeks ago which very readily might have meant, first, a drain on our gold by foreign countries, and, secondly, as a result of that, a flight of American capital, in the form of gold, out of our country. It is not exaggerating the possibility to tell you that such an occurrence might well have taken from us the major part of our gold reserve and resulted in such a further weakening of our government and private credit as to bring on actual panic conditions and the complete stoppage of the wheels of industry.

The Administration has the definite objective of raising commodity prices to such an extent that those who have borrowed money will, on the average, be able to repay that money in the same kind of dollar which they borrowed. We do not seek to let them get such a cheap dollar that they will be able to pay back a great deal less than they borrowed. In other words, we seek to correct a wrong and not to create another wrong in the opposite direction. That is why powers are being given to the Administration to provide, if necessary, for an enlargement of credit, in order to correct the existing wrong. These powers will be used when, as, and if it may be necessary to accomplish the purpose.

Hand in hand with the domestic situation which, of course, is our first concern, is the world situation, and I want to emphasize to you that the domestic situation is inevitably and deeply tied in with the conditions in all of the other nations of the world. In other words, we can get, in all probability, a fair measure of prosperity return in the United States, but it will not be permanent unless we get a return to prosperity all over the world.

In the conferences which we have held and are holding with the leaders of other nations, we are seeking four great objectives: First, a general reduction of armaments and through this the removal of the fear of invasion and armed attack, and, at the same time, a reduction in armament costs, in order to help in the balancing of government budgets and the reduction of taxation. Second, a cutting down of the trade barriers, in order to restart the flow of exchange of crops and goods among nations. Third, the setting up of a stabilization of currencies, in order that trade can make contracts ahead. Fourth, the re-establishment of friendly relations and greater confidence among all nations.

Our foreign visitors these past three weeks have responded to these purposes in a very helpful way. All of the nations have suffered alike in this great depression. They have all reached the conclusion that each can best be helped by the common action of all. It is in this spirit that our visitors have met with us and discussed our common problems. The international conference that lies before us must succeed. The future of the world demands it and we have each of us pledged ourselves to the best joint efforts to this end.

To you, the people of this country, all of us, the Members of the Congress and the members of this Administration owe a profound debt of gratitude. Throughout the depression you have been patient. You have granted us wide powers, you have encouraged us with a widespread approval of our purposes. Every ounce of strength and every resource at our command we have devoted to the end of justifying your confidence. We are encouraged to believe that a wise and sensible beginning has been made. In the present spirit of mutual confidence and mutual encouragement we go forward.

In connection with the new legislation, many things had to be developed by actual experience. For example, the first regulations for compensation of service-connected World War veterans with specific injuries had cut deeper than was originally intended. Early in May, many of the regulations and schedules were redrafted to bring about more equitable treatment.

When the Farm Relief Bill, relating to the refinancing of farm debts, was signed on May twelfth, I made a special appeal to mortgage creditors and others having claims against farmers, that they abstain from bringing foreclosure proceedings, and asking them to co-operate with those who were putting the new machinery into effect.

Also, when on May twelfth, I signed the appropriation bill granting five hundred million dollars for unemployment relief, I tried to make it very clear that this would not absolve States and local communities from their responsibility to do everything within their power to provide the necessities of life for their citizens who were in destitute circumstances.

Again and again, it has been necessary to re-iterate the principle that the first obligation is on the locality; that when the locality has done its utmost and still more must be done, the next obligation is on the State: that only after State and local governments have done their full share can the Federal Government come forward with Federal funds. This is as true in the spring of 1934 as it was in the spring of 1933. It is an unfortunate fact that some people who are the first to cry out against Federal expenditures, are the last people to insist in their own home communities that every possible local effort must be made to prevent destitution and want.

CHAPTER SEVEN

I T WOULD not be fair to say that the National Recovery Act was proposed as a last-minute happy thought, any more than it would be to say that it was thought out and planned for before the new Administration came in.

As far back as the autumn of 1930, I had begun to discuss ways and means for the relief of unemployment and for the reconstituting of our economic machinery. This involved, of course, a complete survey not only of agriculture and industry and finance, but also of the social needs of the whole Nation.

Even at that time plans of all kinds commenced coming to me by mail and through individuals and delegations. With the help of many friends, honest study was given to every one of these plans which seemed to hold out some new thought or some grouping of thoughts which might fit into a comprehensive, and at the same time, a practical unit.

A careful digest of plans and a careful appraisal,

both of public opinion and of government finance, led me to a decision which involved the use of two simultaneous methods.

The first method sought to apply to industry a concept new in our history. The transfer of national supremacy from the agricultural population to the owners of industry and finance which took place at the turn of the century, together with the creation of great concentrations of business management, had led a generation ago to what we called the attack on the trusts.

After the World War, a wholly unplanned pyramiding of production and of speculation had left the country in such condition that methods of recovery used in previous periods of depression were useless.

It is not stretching the point to state categorically that there was not a major industry in the United States in the spring of 1933 that was not suffering either from over-production, or destructive competition, or unfair practices, or complete lack of planning. Industry itself blamed the anti-trust laws. Industry was wrong. The anti-trust laws were aimed at the prevention of monopolies which through restraint of trade would prevent honest competition and gouge the public.

I suppose it is human nature for business men, like other men, to be selfish when business is good and they are making handsome profits. I suppose it is also human for business men, like other men, in times of dire distress when everything is going wrong to be very ready to agree to some new plan which they hope will make things right.

In any event, the overwhelming majority of the business men in May, 1933, were entirely willing to go along with a great co-operative movement directed by the Government and working towards the elimination of the costly practices of the past.

I thought it necessary to differentiate to a certain extent between various industries because of the greatly varying conditions in the actual operations of industries. We had for many weeks, and indeed months, subscribed to the general principle that if the hours of labor for the individual could be shortened, more people would be employed on a given piece of work. That was the purpose behind Senator Black's bill that called for a thirty-hour week for all employees in every industry and in every part of the country. Closer study, however, led us to believe that while the ultimate objective might be sound, the convulsive reorganization necessary to put such a law into effect might do almost as much harm as it would good.

Furthermore, I believed and still believe, that the objectives could be attained with the co-operation of business itself in working out an evolutionary process that called for the co-operation of employees and of labor in developing for each industry what has since become known as codes. Through such co-operation, we thought that wide re-employment would result through the shortening of the working week, that child labor could be eliminated and that a decent minimum wage could be guaranteed to every worker.

In other words, we sought to do for labor by co-operation what the State governments and the Federal Government had failed to accomplish by legislation over a period of many years.

Such was the genesis, such was the purpose of what we called Title I of the National Recovery Act—a great act which, with the Agricultural Adjustment Act, stands in the first rank in the program of rebuilding America.

The second part related to putting people back to work by direct government action, to relieving distress and to building up national purchasing power.

Many people had advocated the appropriation of vast sums running as high as five billion dollars, or even more, to be spent on a program of public works. All of us were in favor of public works on a great scale; but I had made up my mind that public works for the mere sake of spending money could not be justified by us or by future generations. To put a thousand men to work with picks and shovels to dig up a water main on one side of a highway, and lay it again on the other side of the highway, is not only a silly project but it destroys the morale of the men who are doing the job. To find useful public works meant, of necessity, a limit to the amount that could be spent. Almost every government agency, especially those of municipalities, had been using for three years past their own unemployed on all kinds of local projects.

We went over the field with care and came to the conclusion that a sum in the neighborhood of three billion dollars was about all that we could allocate usefully in one year. This sum included highway construction to the extent of nearly half a billion dollars; Navy building to commence catching up with our London Treaty naval strength; approximately, a billion dollars for great Federal projects principally concerned with flood control and inland navigation; and finally, allocations to States and counties and municipalities by way of part loan and part grant.

This was the objective of Title II of the National Recovery Act which appropriated three billion, three hundred million dollars for public works.

At the same time, in order to maintain the credit of the Federal Government, I proposed sufficient taxes to pay the interest on and amortize this huge expenditure.

The message to Congress of May seventeenth speaks for itself:

Before the Special Session of the Congress adjourns, I recommend two further steps in our national campaign to put people to work.

My first request is that—the Congress provide for the machinery necessary for a great co-operative movement throughout all industry in order to obtain wide re-employment, to shorten the working week, to pay a decent wage for the shorter week and to prevent unfair competition and disastrous over-production.

Employers cannot do this singly or even in organized groups, because such action increases costs and thus permits cut-throat underselling by selfish competitors unwilling to join in such a public-spirited endeavor.

One of the great restrictions upon such co-operative efforts up to this time has been our anti-trust laws. They were properly designed as the means to cure the great evils of monopolistic price fixing.

They should certainly be retained as a permanent assurance that the old evils of unfair competition shall never return. But the public interest will be served if, with the authority and under the guidance of government, private industries are permitted to make agreements and codes insuring fair competition. However, it is necessary, if we thus limit the operation of anti-trust laws to their original purpose to provide a rigorous licensing power in order to meet rare cases of non-co-operation and abuse. Such a safeguard is indispensable.

The other proposal gives the Executive full power to start a large program of direct employment. A careful survey convinces me that approximately $3,300,000,000 can be invested in useful and necessary public construction, and at the same time put the largest possible number of people to work.

Provision should be made to permit States, counties and municipalities to undertake useful public works, subject, however, to the most effective possible means of eliminating favoritism and wasteful expenditures on unwarranted and uneconomic projects.

We must, by prompt and vigorous action, override unnecessary obstructions which in the past have delayed the starting of public works programs. This can be accomplished by simple and direct procedure.

In carrying out this program it is imperative that the credit of the United States Government be protected and preserved. This means that at the same time we are making these vast emergency expenditures there must be provided sufficient revenue to pay interest and amortization on the cost and that the revenues so provided must be adequate and certain rather than inadequate and speculative.

Careful estimates indicate that at least $220,-000,000 of additional revenue will be required to service the contemplated borrowings of the Government. This will of necessity involve some form or forms of new taxation. A number of suggestions have been made as to the nature of these taxes. I do not make a specific recommendation at this time, but I hope that the Committee on Ways and Means of the House of Representatives, will make a careful study of revenue plans and be prepared by the beginning of the coming week to propose the taxes which they judge to be best adapted to meet the present need and which will at the same time be least burdensome to our people. At the end of that time, if no decision has been reached or if the means proposed do not seem to be sufficiently adequate or certain, it is my intention to transmit to the Congress my own recommendations in the matter.

The taxes to be imposed are for the purpose of providing re-employment for our citizens. Provision should be made for their reduction or elimination—

First—As fast as increasing revenues from improving business become available to replace them;

Second—Whenever the repeal of the Eighteenth Amendment now pending before the States shall have been ratified and the repeal of the Volstead Act effected. The pre-Prohibition revenue laws would then automatically go into effect and yield enough wholly to eliminate these temporary re-employment taxes.

Finally, I stress the fact that all of these proposals are based on the gravity of the emergency and that therefore it is urgently necessary immediately to initiate a re-employment campaign if we are to avoid further hardships, to sustain business improvement and to pass on to better things.

For this reason I urge prompt action on this legislation.

On June tenth, the Executive Order was issued which, for the first time, consolidated the purchase of almost all government supplies, except those of the Army and Navy, in a procurement division set up in the Treasury Department; and at the same time the disbursing offices of the many government departments were consolidated in a central disbursement division in the Treasury Department.

CHAPTER EIGHT

FROM this time on to the end of the Session, there was little in the way of new recommendations. On May twentieth, I asked that the oil industry be included as a separate entity in whatever action the Congress decided to take in regard to the other industries.

On June sixth, further changes were announced by Executive Order in relation to the regulations governing the cuts in veterans' compensation. Payments to men suffering from specific and serious injuries were increased. The older Spanish War veterans' pay was also increased and many other upward adjustments were allowed in order to correct cuts which in the first instance undoubtedly had been too drastic.

On June tenth, I advised the Congress of a number of consolidations and transfers of duties within government departments and agencies, estimating that the savings thereby would amount to twenty-five million dollars annually.

The Emergency Relief Act had been passed. We held a splendid meeting of all the State administrators at the White House on June fourteenth. The following statement gave to them the purposes of the new Federal Relief Administration:

The Emergency Relief Act is an expression of the Federal Government's determination to co-operate with the States and local communities with regard to financing emergency relief work. It means just that. It is essential that the States and local units of government do their fair share. They must not expect the Federal Government to finance more than a reasonable proportion of the total. It should be borne in mind by the State authorities and by the five thousand local relief committees, now functioning throughout the land, that there are four million families in need of the necessities of life.

Obviously the Federal Relief Administrator should put as much responsibility as possible on the State Administration. This means a competent set-up in each State, preferably a commission of five or six well-known citizens, who will not only administer the relief in a business-like way but entirely apart from partisan politics. The only way relief officials can be assured that people are getting relief who need relief is to have competent administration.

It is essential that there be effective co-ordination of relief and public works in all communities. While an important factor in setting up a public works program is speed, there is no intention of using the public works funds simply to build a lot of useless projects disguised as relief. It is the purpose to encourage real public works. One function of public works in an emergency is to provide a bridge by which people can pass from relief status over to normal self-support. Partisan politics must play no part in the carrying out of this work. The use of public works as a means of rational redistribution of population from congested centers to more wholesome surroundings where people can have a chance to lead normal life will be encouraged.

It is a primary purpose of my administration to co-operate with the States and with industry to secure work opportunities for as many of the unemployed as possible, by which they will find employment through normal channels. But until those jobs are available the Federal Government, States and every local community must provide relief for every genuinely needy unemployed person in America.

I know that I can count on your full and complete co-operation with the Federal Emergency Relief Administrator and I can assure you on his behalf of a sympathetic understanding of your problems and of decisive action when that is necessary.

During the closing days of that Special Session of the Seventy-third Congress, a very definite attempt was made in the Senate to destroy, at least in part, a fundamental principle established as a result of the Economy Act. This effort would have re-enacted, by law, presumptions that subsequent illness of veterans was the result of and caused by war service. I took the firm position that presumption is a question of fact and not of law, and that each case ought to be decided on the merits of the individual case. Finally, we came to an agreement that District Boards should examine every case and determine the fact in as fair a way as possible. Later, I set up a Special Board of Appeals composed, in a large part like the District Boards, of veterans themselves.

Bills were coming down from the Capitol at frequent intervals and each had to be carefully checked before signing.

The new National Recovery Administration had to be set up and also the Public Works Administration and the Oil Administration.

Before leaving Washington on June seventeenth I gave out the following statements about the Recovery Act, which I think are worth reprinting because so much of our future history will date back to this moment:

History probably will record the National Industrial Recovery Act as the most important and far-reaching legislation ever enacted by the American Congress. It represents a supreme effort to stabilize for all time the many factors which make for the prosperity of the Nation, and the preservation of American standards.

Its goal is the assurance of a reasonable profit to industry and living wages for labor with the elimination of the piratical methods and practices which have not only harassed honest business but also contributed to the ills of labor.

While we are engaged in establishing new foundations for business which ultimately should open a return to work for large numbers of men, it is our hope through the so-called Public Works section of the law to speedily initiate a program of public construction that should early re-employ additional hundreds of thousands of men.

Obviously, if this project is to succeed, it demands the whole-hearted co-operation of industry, labor and every citizen of the nation.

The law I have just signed was passed *to put people back to work*—to let them buy more of the products of farms and factories and start our business at a living rate again. This task is in two stages—first, to get many hundreds of thousands of the unemployed back on the payroll by snowfall and second, to plan for a better future for the longer pull. While we shall not neglect the second, the first stage is an emergency job. It has the right of way.

The second part of the act gives employment by a vast program of public works. Our studies show that we should be able to hire many men at once and to step up to about a million new jobs by October first, and a much greater number later. We must put at the head of our list those works which are fully ready to start now. Our first purpose is to create employment as fast as we can but we should not pour money into unproved projects.

We have worked out our plans for action. Some of it will start tomorrow. I am making available four hundred million dollars for State roads under regulations which I have just signed and I am told that the States will get this work under way at once. I have also just released over $200,000,000 for the Navy to start building ships under the London Treaty.

In my inaugural I laid down the simple proposition that nobody is going to starve in this country. It seems to me to be equally plain that no business which depends for existence on paying less than living wages to its workers has any right to continue in this country. By "business" I mean the whole of commerce as well as the whole of industry; by workers I mean all workers—the white-collar class as well as the men in overalls; and by *living* wages I mean more than a bare subsistence level—I mean the wages of *decent* living.

Throughout industry, the change from starvation wages and starvation employment to living wages and sustained employment can, in large part, be made by an industrial covenant to which all employers shall subscribe. It is greatly to their interest to do this because decent living, widely spread among our 125,000,000 people, eventually means the opening up to industry of the richest market which the world has known. It is the only way to utilize the so-called excess capacity of our industrial plants. This is the principle that makes this one of the most important laws that ever came from Congress because, before the passage of this Act, no such industrial covenant was possible.

On this idea, the first part of the Act proposes to our industry a great spontaneous co-operation to put millions of men back in their regular jobs this summer. The idea is simply for employers to hire more men to do the existing work by reducing work-hours of each man's week, and at the same time paying a living wage for the shorter week.

No employer and no group of less than all employers in a single trade could do this alone and

99

continue to live in business competition. But if *all* employers in each trade now band themselves faithfully in these modern guilds—without exception—and agree to act together and at once, none will be hurt and millions of workers, so long deprived of the right to earn their bread in the sweat of their labor, can raise their heads again. The challenge of this law is whether we can sink selfish interest and present a solid front against a common peril.

It is a challenge to industry which has long insisted that, given the right to act in unison, it could do much for the general good which has hitherto been unlawful. From today it has that right.

Many good men voted this new charter with misgivings. I do not share these doubts. I had part in the great co-operation of 1917 and 1918 and it is my faith that we can count on our industry once more to join in our general purpose to lift this new threat and to do it without taking any advantage of the public trust which has this day been reposed without stint in the good faith and high purpose of American business.

But industry is challenged in another way. It is not only the slackers within trade groups who may stand in the path of our common purpose. In a sense these groups compete with each other, and no single industry, and no separate cluster of industries, can do this job alone for exactly the same reason that no single employer can do it alone. In other words, we can imagine such a thing as a *slacker industry*.

This law is also a challenge to labor. Workers, too, are here given a new charter of rights long sought and hitherto denied. But they know that the first move expected by the nation is a great co-operation of all employers, by one single mass-action, to improve the case of workers on a scale never attempted in any nation. Industries can do this only if they have the support of the whole public and especially of their own workers. This is not a law to foment discord and it will not be executed as such. This is a time for mutual confidence and help and we can safely rely on the sense of fair play among all Americans to assure every industry which now moves forward promptly in this united drive against depression that its workers will be with it to a man.

It is, further, a challenge to administration. We are relaxing some of the safeguards of the anti-trust laws. The public must be protected against the abuses that led to their enactment, and to this end, we are putting in place of old principles of unchecked competition some new government controls. They must above all be impartial and just. Their purpose is to free business—not to shackle it—and no man who stands on the constructive forward-looking side of his industry has anything to fear from them. To such men the opportunities for individual initiative will open more amply than ever. Let me make it clear, however, that the anti-trust laws still stand firmly against monopolies that restrain trade and price fixing which allows inordinate profits or unfairly high prices.

If we ask our trade groups to do that which exposes their business, as never before, to undermining by members who are unwilling to do their parts, we must guard those who play the game for the general good against those who may seek selfish gains from the unselfishness of others. We must protect them from the racketeers who invade organizations of both employers and workers. We are spending billions of dollars and if that spending is really to serve our ends it must be done quickly. We must see that our haste does not permit favoritism and graft. All this is a heavy load for any Government and one that can be borne only if we have the patience, co-operation, and support of people everywhere.

Finally, this law is a challenge to our whole people. There is no power in America that can force against the public will such action as we require. But there is no group in America that can withstand the force of an aroused public opinion. This great co-operation can succeed only if those who bravely go forward to restore jobs have aggressive public support and those who lag are made to feel the full weight of public disapproval.

As to the machinery—the practical way of accomplishing what we are setting out to do, when a trade association has a code ready to submit and the association has qualified as truly representative, and after reasonable notice has been issued to all concerned, a public hearing will be held by the Administrator or a deputy. A labor Advisory Board appointed by the Secretary of Labor will be responsible that every affected labor group, whether organized or unorganized, is fully and adequately represented in an advisory capacity and any interested labor group will be entitled to be heard through representatives of its own choosing. An Industrial Advisory Board appointed by the Secretary of Commerce will be responsible that every affected industrial group is fully and adequately represented in an advisory capacity and any interested industrial group will be entitled to be heard through representatives of its own choosing. A Consumers' Advisory Board will be responsible that the interests of the consuming public will be represented and every reasonable opportunity will be given to any group or class who may be affected directly or indirectly to present their views.

At the conclusion of these hearings and after the most careful scrutiny by a competent economic staff the Administrator will present the subject to me for my action under the law.

I am fully aware that wage increases will eventually raise costs, but I ask that managements give first consideration to the improvement of operating figures by greatly increased sales to be expected from the rising purchasing power of the public.

That is good economics and good business. The aim of this whole effort is to restore our rich domestic market by raising its vast consuming capacity. If we now inflate prices as fast and as far as we increase wages, the whole project will be set at naught. We cannot hope for the full effect of this plan unless, in these first critical months, and, even at the expense of full initial profits, we defer price increases as long as possible. If we can thus start a strong sound upward spiral of business activity our industries will have little doubt of black-ink operations in the last quarter of this year. The pent-up demand of this people is very great and if we can release it on so broad a front, we need not fear a lagging recovery. There is greater danger of too much feverish speed.

In a few industries, there has been some forward buying at unduly depressed prices in recent weeks. Increased costs resulting from this Government-inspired movement may make it very hard for some manufacturers and jobbers to fulfill some of their present contracts without loss. It will be a part of this wide industrial co-operation for those having the benefit of these forward bargains (contracted before the law was passed) to take the initiative in revising them to absorb some share of the increase in their suppliers' costs, thus raised in the public interest. It is only in such a willing and considerate spirit, throughout the whole of industry, that we can hope to succeed.

Under Title I of this Act, I have appointed

Hugh Johnson as Administrator and a special Industrial Recovery Board under the Chairmanship of the Secretary of Commerce. This organization is now prepared to receive proposed Codes and to conduct prompt hearings looking toward their submission to me for approval. While acceptable proposals of no trade group will be delayed, it is my hope that the ten major industries which control the bulk of industrial employment can submit their simple basic Codes at once and that the country can look forward to the month of July as the beginning of our great national movement back to work.

During the coming three weeks Title II relating to public works and construction projects will be temporarily conducted by Colonel Donald H. Sawyer as Administrator and a special temporary board consisting of the Secretary of the Interior as Chairman, the Secretary of Commerce, the Secretary of Agriculture, the Secretary of War, the Attorney General, the Secretary of Labor and the Director of the Budget.

During the next two weeks the Administrator and this board will make a study of all projects already submitted or to be submitted and, as previously stated, certain allotments under the new law will be made immediately.

Between these twin efforts—public works and industrial re-employment—it is not too much to expect that a great many men and women can be taken from the ranks of the unemployed before winter comes. It is the most important attempt of this kind in history. As in the great crisis of the World War, it puts a whole people to the simple but vital test:—*"Must we go on in many groping, disorganized, separate units to defeat or shall we move as one great team to victory?"*

It was of course obvious that it would take several weeks to set up the necessary machinery, but the start had to be made that same day. General Hugh S. Johnson was appointed Administrator for Industrial Recovery under Title I of the Act and he, acting with a Special Industrial Recovery Board, composed of the Secretary of Commerce, the Attorney General, Secretary of the Interior, Secretary of Agriculture, Secretary of Labor, the Director of the Budget, and the Chairman of the Federal Trade Commission were charged with putting the Act into effect.

On June twenty-sixth, I delegated to the Secretary of Agriculture all of the functions relating to agriculture authorized under Title I of the National Recovery Act. Under this power Secretary of Agriculture Wallace appointed Mr. George Peek and set up the organization of the Agricultural Adjustment Administration.

At the same time, a Special Board for Public Works consisting of Colonel Donald H. Sawyer, as temporary Administrator, together with the Secretary of the Interior, the Secretary of War, the Attorney General, Secretary of Agriculture, Secretary of Commerce, Director of the Budget,

Colonel George R. Spalding and Assistant Secretary of the Treasury Robert was charged with setting up the Public Works Administration to administer Title II of the Act.

In the early hours of June sixteenth, the Congress adjourned. I am happy once more to pay tribute to the members of the Senate and House of Representatives of both parties who so generously and loyally co-operated with me in the solution of our joint problems.

I shall always remember June 16, 1933. There were farewells to be said to the Vice President, the Speaker, and members of the Senate and House.

I am certain that this Special Session of the Congress will go down in the history of our country as one which, more than any other, boldly seized the opportunity to right great wrongs, to restore clearer thinking and more honest practices, to carry through its business with practical celerity and to set our feet on the upward path.

I had hoped to get away that night to see my son who was graduating from school and to proceed on a cruise along the New England Coast on a small schooner.

With all letters answered and all work up to date, as far as a President's work can ever be up to date, I left on Friday Evening, June seventeenth, for salt water.

CHAPTER NINE

IN FOREIGN, even more than in domestic affairs, a nation needs to have a basic continuing policy. World peace is thus strengthened because each nation can thereby rely more permanently on the actions of its neighbors. World unrest, world distrust arise in great part from the uncertainties of foreign policies and the lack of adherence to definite and unselfish principles.

Foreign policies must, of necessity, be put into words by the heads of the respective governments and this fact has been a reason why so often international policies have represented the ambitions of individual leaders or the machinations of special groups rather than the real purpose and desires of the people themselves within any given country.

Our own official relationship to the rest of the world has by no means been consistent through the past century and a half; and yet, I am convinced that the American people as a whole have had a far more consistent policy than many of their leaders or administrations.

I have sought, therefore, to approach the problem of our foreign relations in what I believe to be the underlying spirit of the great majority of people in every part of our country.

Instead of taking up the various steps in our dealings with other nations in the thread of this general narrative, I am placing them together in this separate chapter. Nevertheless, they should be read in the light of our own successive domestic, legislative and administrative steps taken throughout this first year. This is especially true of the events leading up to and through the London Economic Conference.

In my Inaugural Address, I had referred briefly to foreign affairs, stressing the thought that the fundamental of American foreign policy should be that of "the good neighbor." The first opportunity which I had to develop this thought was at the special session of the Governing Board of the Pan American Union on April twelfth. In the following address, I sought to express, in simple terms, what the relationships of the twenty-one republics of America should be to each other:

I rejoice in this opportunity to participate in the celebration of "Pan American Day" and to extend on behalf of the people of the United States a fraternal greeting to our sister American Republics. The celebration of "Pan American Day" in this building, dedicated to international goodwill and co-operation, exemplifies a unity of thought and purpose among the peoples of this hemisphere. It is a manifestation of the common ideal of mutual helpfulness, sympathetic understanding and spiritual solidarity.

There is inspiration in the thought that on this day the attention of the citizens of the twenty-one republics of America is focused on the common ties—historical, cultural, economic and social—which bind them to one another. Common ideals and a community of interest, together with a spirit of co-operation, have led to the realization that the well-being of one nation depends in large measure upon the well-being of its neighbors. It is upon these foundations that Pan Americanism has been built.

This celebration commemorates a movement based upon the policy of fraternal co-operation. In my Inaugural Address I stated that I would "dedicate this nation to the policy of the good neighbor—the neighbor who resolutely respects himself and, because he does so, respects the rights of others—the neighbor who respects his obligations and respects the sanctity of his agreements in and with a world of neighbors." Never before has the significance of the word "good neighbor" been so manifest in international relations. Never have the need and benefit of neighborly co-operation in every form of human activity been so evident as they are today.

Friendship among nations, as among individuals, calls for constructive efforts to muster the forces of humanity in order that an atmosphere of close understanding and co-operation may be cultivated. It involves mutual obligations and responsibilities, for it is only by sympathetic respect for the rights of others and a scrupulous fulfillment of the corresponding obligations by each member of the community that a true fraternity can be maintained.

The essential qualities of a true Pan Americanism must be the same as those which constitute a good neighbor, namely, mutual understanding, and, through such understanding, a sympathetic appreciation of the other's point of view. It is only in this manner that we can hope to build up a system of which confidence, friendship and good-will are the cornerstones.

In this spirit the people of every republic on our continent are coming to a deep understanding of the fact that the Monroe Doctrine, of which so much has been written and spoken for more than a century, was and is directed at the maintenance of independence by the peoples of the continent. It was aimed and is aimed against the acquisition in any manner of the control of additional territory in this hemisphere by any non-American power.

Hand in hand with this Pan American doctrine of continental self-defense, the peoples of the American Republics understand more clearly, with the passing years, that the independence of each republic must recognize the independence of every other republic. Each one of us must grow by an advancement of civilization and social well-being and not by the acquisition of territory at the expense of any neighbor.

In this spirit of mutual understanding and of co-operation on this continent you and I cannot fail to be disturbed by any armed strife between neighbors. I do not hesitate to say to you, the distinguished members of the Governing Board of the Pan American Union, that I regard existing conflicts between four of our sister republics as a backward step.

Your Americanism and mine must be a structure built of confidence, cemented by a sympathy which recognizes only equality and fraternity. It finds its source and being in the hearts of men and dwells in the temple of the intellect.

We all of us have peculiar problems, and, to speak frankly, the interest of our own citizens must, in each instance, come first. But it is equally true that it is of vital importance to every nation of this continent that the American Governments, individually, take, without further delay, such action as may be possible to abolish all unnecessary and artificial barriers and restrictions which now hamper the healthy flow of trade between the peoples of the American Republics.

I am glad to deliver this message to you, Gentlemen of the Governing Board of the Pan American Union, for I look upon the union as the outward expression of the spiritual unity of the Americas.

It is to this unity which must be courageous and vital in its elements that humanity must look for one of the great stabilizing influences in world affairs.

In closing, may I refer to the ceremony which is to take place a little later in the morning at which the Government of Venezuela will present to the Pan American Union the bust of a great American leader and patriot, Francisco de Miranda. I join with you in this tribute.

Later developments in our Pan American relationships did not occur until the time of the troubles in Cuba in the late summer.

Early in April conversations between the principal nations of the world in regard to the coming International Economic Conference were held. When this great gathering was proposed a year before it was rightly thought that it would afford an opportunity for free and wholesome discussion of a large number of economic, financial, commercial and social problems. A special committee had prepared a most interesting program covering many matters. I think it is fair to say that the principal objective was the exploration of ways and means for breaking down all kinds of trade barriers, for developing the interchange of goods and agricultural products between nations—in other words, for building up world trade. Financial and monetary problems were, to be sure, a part of this program but only a part, and stabilization of existing exchange rates between England, France and the United States formed but a fraction of this part.

It was in the spirit of examining the whole program that I invited many national leaders to come to Washington in April and May. We were honored by visits from Prime Minister MacDonald of Great Britain, Prime Minister Bennett of Canada, Monsieur Herriot of France, Finance Minister Jung of Italy, Ambassador Le Breton of the Argentine Republic, Finance Minister Schacht of Germany, Finance Minister Pani of Mexico, Finance Minister Soong of China, Senhor Brasil of Brazil, Viscount Ishii of Japan, Señor Torres of Chili and gentlemen representing other nations in a diplomatic capacity in Washington.

Our conversations were on broad lines, relating to many subjects; they were in no sense confined to stabilization of the pound, franc and dollar; they related far more to the breaking down of trade barriers by reciprocal and other methods, and the visualization and application of world remedies to world problems. I am making this clear at this point in view of the later happenings in London, and in view of the crisis which was developing in the World Disarmament Conference then in progress at Geneva.

That conference, organized under the auspices

of the League of Nations, but wholly distinct from the League, had had the enthusiastic backing of the American Government from its inception. It had made progress, and was engaged in actual discussion of a concrete program which, in respect to existing land armies and armaments, proposed over a period of years a reduction of the man power of those armies and of the weapons of attack.

Early in May, it seemed clear that these conversations were about to be disrupted by the attitude of the German Government and by putting forward of European political and racial difficulties at the expense of the wider world purpose.

I felt that an appeal to the heads of governments throughout the world would be useful at this time, not only in preventing a break-up of the Disarmament Conference, but also in setting forth a clear, definite and practical principle as the goal for continuing the work. The following message had at least the merit of pouring oil on troubled waters:

A profound hope of the people of my country impels me, as the head of their Government, to address you and, through you, the people of your nation. This hope is that peace may be assured through practical measures of disarmament and that all of us may carry to victory our common struggle against economic chaos.

To these ends the nations have called two great world conferences. The happiness, the prosperity and the very lives of the men, women and children who inhabit the whole world are bound up in the decisions which their governments will make in the near future. The improvement of social conditions, the preservation of individual human rights and the furtherance of social justice are dependent upon these decisions.

The World Economic Conference will meet soon and must come to its conclusions quickly. The world cannot await deliberations long drawn out. The conference must establish order in place of the present chaos by a stabilization of currencies, by freeing the flow of world trade and by international action to raise price levels. It must, in short, supplement individual domestic programs for economic recovery by wise and considered international action.

The Disarmament Conference has labored for more than a year and, as yet, has been unable to reach satisfactory conclusions. Confused purposes still clash dangerously. Our duty lies in the direction of bringing practical results through concerted action based upon the greatest good to the greatest number. Before the imperative call of this great duty, petty obstacles must be swept away and petty aims forgotten. A selfish victory is always destined to be an ultimate defeat. The furtherance of durable peace for our generation in every part of the world is the only goal worthy of our best efforts.

If we ask what are the reasons for armaments, which, in spite of the lessons and tragedies of the World War, are today a greater burden on the peoples of the earth than ever before, it becomes clear that they are two-fold: First, the desire, disclosed or hidden, on the part of governments to enlarge their territories at the expense of a sister nation. I believe that only a small minority of governments or of peoples harbor such a purpose. Second, the fear of nations that they will be invaded. I believe that the overwhelming majority of peoples feel obliged to retain excessive armaments because they fear some act of aggression against them and not because they themselves seek to be aggressors.

There is justification for this fear. Modern weapons of offense are vastly stronger than modern weapons of defense. Frontier forts, trenches, wire entanglements, coast defenses—in a word, fixed fortifications—are no longer impregnable to the attack of war planes, heavy mobile artillery, land battleships called tanks and poison gas.

If all nations will agree wholly to eliminate from possession and use the weapons which make possible a successful attack, defenses automatically will become impregnable, and the frontiers and independence of every nation will become secure.

The ultimate objective of the Disarmament Conference must be the complete elimination of all offensive weapons. The immediate objective is a substantial reduction of some of these weapons and the elimination of many others.

This Government believes that the program for immediate reduction of aggressive weapons, now under discussion at Geneva, is but a first step toward our ultimate goal. We do not believe that the proposed immediate steps go far enough. Nevertheless, this Government welcomes the measures now proposed and will exert its influence toward the attainment of further successive steps of disarmament.

Stated in the clearest way, there are three steps to be agreed upon in the present discussions:

First: to take, at once, the first definite step toward this objective, as broadly outlined in the MacDonald Plan.

Second: to agree upon time and procedure for taking the following steps.

Third: to agree that while the first and the following steps are being taken, no nation shall increase its existing armaments over and above the limitations of treaty obligations.

But the peace of the world must be assured during the whole period of disarmament and I, therefore, propose a fourth step concurrent with and wholly dependent on the faithful fulfillment of these three proposals and subject to existing treaty rights:

That all the nations of the world should enter

into a solemn and definite pact of non-aggression: That they should solemnly reaffirm the obligations they have assumed to limit and reduce their armaments, and, provided these obligations are faithfully executed by all signatory powers, individually agree that they will send no armed force of whatsoever nature across their frontiers.

Common sense points out that if any strong nation refuses to join with genuine sincerity in these concerted efforts for political and economic peace, the one at Geneva and the other at London, progress can be obstructed and ultimately blocked. In such event the civilized world, seeking both forms of peace, will know where the responsibility for failure lies. I urge that no nation assume such a responsibility, and that all the nations joined in these great conferences translate their professed policies into action. This is the way to political and economic peace.

I trust that your government will join in the fulfillment of these hopes.

At the same time, I informed the Congress of what I had done in the following message:

For the information of the Congress I am sending herewith a message that I have addressed this morning to the sovereigns and presidents of those nations participating in the Disarmament Conference and the World Monetary and Economic Conference.

I was impelled to this action because it has become increasingly evident that the assurance of world political and economic peace and stability is threatened by selfish and short-sighted policies, actions and threats of actions.

The sincere wish for this assurance by an overwhelming majority of the nations faces the danger of recalcitrant obstruction by a very small minority, just as in the domestic field the good purposes of a majority in business, labor or in other cooperative efforts are often frustrated by a selfish few.

The deep-rooted desire of Americans for better living conditions and for the avoidance of war is shared by mass humanity in every country. As a means to this end I have, in the message to the various nations, stressed the practical necessity of reducing armaments. It is high time for us and for every other nation to understand the simple fact that the invasion of any nation, or the destruction of a national sovereignty, can be prevented only by the complete elimination of the weapons that make such a course possible today.

Such an elimination will make the little nation relatively more secure against the great nation.

Furthermore, permanent defenses are a nonrecurring charge against governmental budgets while large armies, continually rearmed with improved offensive weapons, constitute a recurring charge. This, more than any other factor today, is responsible for governmental deficits and threatened bankruptcy.

The way to disarm is to disarm. The way to prevent invasion is to make it impossible.

I have asked for an agreement among nations on four practical and simultaneous steps:

First: that through a series of steps the weapons of offensive warfare be eliminated;

Second: that the first definite step be taken now;

Third: that while these steps are being taken no nation shall increase existing armaments over and above the limitations of treaty obligations;

Fourth: that subject to existing treaty rights no nation during the disarmament period shall send any armed force of whatsoever nature across its own borders.

Our people realize that weapons of offense are needed only if other nations have them and they will freely give them up if all the nations of the world will do likewise.

In the domestic field the Congress has labored in sympathetic understanding with me for the improvement of social conditions, for the preservation of individual human rights and for the furtherance of social justice.

In the message to the nations which I herewith transmit I have named the same objectives. It is in order to assure these great human values that we seek peace by ridding the world of the weapons of aggression and attack.

It is with a profound feeling of regret that today, late in February, 1934, many months later, we cannot record substantial gain in the progress of the work of the Disarmament Conference. Unwillingness of some governments and, I regret to say, of some peoples to abandon the thought or the purpose of territorial expansion or imperial aggrandizement means that the United States can only repeat its willingness to join the other nations as soon as they agree to a realistic and useful disarmament plan. Our Nation stands ready to enter into any world pact which will equitably and fairly reduce armaments and free the world population from strangling expenditures and from the constant dread of invasion and attack.

Returning briefly to the Economic Conference, the American Delegation headed by Secretary of State Hull left Washington late in May. Very soon after their arrival it became clear that the delegations of certain nations in the conference were determined to compel some definite and immediate form of stabilization of the exchange rate between the dollar, the franc and the pound, as a condition precedent to the serious discussion of any of the many other objectives of the conference.

Rumors to this effect became so insistent that Secretary of the Treasury Woodin found it necessary to issue the following statement on June fifteenth:

Various reports from London published today concerning an agreement by American delegates to stabilization in some form have been brought to my attention. Such reports cannot be founded in fact.

Any proposal concerning stabilization would have to be submitted to the President and to the Treasury and no suggestion of such a proposal has been received here. The discussions in London in regard to this subject must be exploratory only and any agreement on this subject will be reached in Washington, not elsewhere.

It is unnecessary further to discuss the details of the conference. The Secretary of State and other members of the American Delegation tried in every way to obtain practical results on other parts of the program. They were able to obtain an agreement relating to the use and purchase of silver. But the demand of the nations constituting what was known as the "gold bloc" amounted to saying to the threescore nations in the conference: "We will not discuss anything; we will break up the conference unless the United States first agrees to immediate exchange stabilization."

This country knew, and all other nations knew, that we were engaged at home in a great program of rehabilitation—a program which called for the raising of values—and that no human being could, at that moment, determine exactly where even a temporary stabilization point should be fixed for the dollar, franc and pound.

Things came to such a pass in London that the need for speaking clearly and unequivocally was so evident that on July second, I dispatched the following message to the Secretary of State and the other members of the American Delegation in London:

I would regard it as a catastrophe amounting to a world tragedy if the great conference of nations, called to bring about a more real and permanent financial stability and a greater prosperity to the masses of all nations, should, in advance of any serious effort to consider these broader problems, allow itself to be diverted by the proposal of a purely artificial and temporary experiment affecting the monetary exchange of a few nations only. Such action, such diversion, shows a singular lack of proportion and a failure to remember the larger purposes for which the Economic Conference originally was called together.

I do not relish the thought that insistence on such action should be made an excuse for the continuance of the basic economic errors that underlie so much of the present world-wide depression.

The world will not long be lulled by the specious fallacy of achieving a temporary and probably an artificial stability in foreign exchange on the part of a few large countries only.

The sound internal economic system of a nation is a greater factor in its well-being than the price of its currency in changing terms of the currencies of other nations.

It is for this reason that reduced cost of government, adequate government income and ability to service government debts are all so important to ultimate stability. So, too, old fetiches of so-called international bankers are being replaced by efforts to plan national currencies with the objective of giving to those currencies a continuing purchasing power which does not greatly vary in terms of the commodities and needs of modern civilization. Let me be frank in saying that the United States seeks the kind of a dollar which a generation hence will have the same purchasing and debt-paying power as the dollar value we hope to attain in the near future. That objective means more to the good of other nations than a fixed ratio for a month or two in terms of the pound or franc.

Our broad purpose is the permanent stabilization of every nation's currency. Gold or gold and silver can well continue to be a metallic reserve behind currencies but this is not the time to dissipate gold reserves. When the world works out concerted policies in the majority of nations to produce balanced budgets and living within their means, then we can properly discuss a better distribution of the world's gold and silver supply to act as a reserve base of national currencies. Restoration of world trade is an important partner, both in the means and in the result. Here also temporary exchange fixing is not the true answer. We must rather mitigate existing embargoes to make easier the exchange of products which one nation has and the other nation has not.

The conference was called to better and perhaps to cure fundamental economic ills. It must not be diverted from that effort.

Secretary Hull, with magnificent force, prevented the conference from final adjournment and made it possible, we all hope, for a renewal of its discussions in the broad field of international relationships.

Internal conditions in Cuba in the first part of August made it necessary to send a few small war ships and coast guard vessels to certain harbors near which Americans were living. The following statement was given out on August thirteenth:

Latest advices are to the effect that domestic disturbances, including acts of violence, are occurring in some parts of Cuba among certain elements of the population.

In these circumstances I feel constrained as a matter of special precaution and solely for the purpose of safeguarding and protecting the lives and persons of American citizens in Cuba, to order certain vessels to points on the Cuban coast.

The change of government now taking place in Cuba is in entire accord with the recognized Constitution and laws of that country, and no possible question of intervention or of the slightest interference with the internal affairs of Cuba has arisen or is intended by this precautionary step to protect, if necessary, the lives of American citizens, pending the restoration of normal conditions of law and order by the Cuban authorities.

I am giving strict instructions accordingly to the Commanders of each vessel.

The American people deeply sympathize with the people of Cuba in their economic distress, and are praying that quiet and strict order may soon prevail in every part of Cuba. The American Government will lend all aid feasible, through constituted Cuban authorities, for the relief of the distressed people of the island.

From this time on a consistent policy of non-intervention was pursued. The United States did not accord formal recognition to the provisional government because we did not feel that it was given sufficiently substantial support by the

Cuban people. In the early part of 1934, however, a new government was constituted under President Mendieta. During Cuba's troubles we kept in close touch with the other American Republics, giving them access to all of our information and cementing, I hope, our frank and friendly relations.

In November a distinguished delegation led by the Secretary of State left for the Conference of American States in Montevideo. The results of this conference were highly gratifying and were heralded throughout the Americas as a success.

Ever since taking office I had felt the absurdity of the inability of the United States to have any relations official or unofficial with Russia. The interchange of the following friendly letters in October paved the way for a visit from M. Litvinoff and the resumption of diplomatic relations with Russia the following month.

THE WHITE HOUSE

Washington, October 10, 1933.

MY DEAR MR. PRESIDENT:

Since the beginning of my administration, I have contemplated the desirability of an effort to end the present abnormal relations between the hundred and twenty-five million people of the United States and the hundred and sixty million people of Russia.

It is most regrettable that these great peoples, between whom a happy tradition of friendship existed for more than a century to their mutual advantage, should now be without a practical method of communicating directly with each other.

The difficulties that have created this anomalous situation are serious but not, in my opinion, insoluble; and difficulties between great nations can be removed only by frank, friendly conversations. If you are of similar mind, I should be glad to receive any representatives you may designate to explore with me personally all questions outstanding between our countries.

Participation in such a discussion would, of course, not commit either nation to any future course of action, but would indicate a sincere desire to reach a satisfactory solution of the problems involved. It is my hope that such conversations might result in good to the people of both our countries.

I am, my dear Mr. President,

Very sincerely yours,

FRANKLIN D. ROOSEVELT.

MR. MIKHAIL KALININ,
*President of the All Union Central
Executive Committee,* Moscow.

MY DEAR MR. PRESIDENT:

I have received your message of October 10th.

I have always considered most abnormal and regrettable a situation wherein, during the past sixteen years, two great republics—The United States of America and the Union of Soviet Socialist Republics—have lacked the usual methods of communication and have been deprived of the benefits which such communication could give. I am glad to note that you also reached the same conclusion.

There is no doubt that difficulties, present or arising, between two countries, can be solved only when direct relations exist between them; and that, on the other hand, they have no chance for solution in the absence of such relations. I shall take the liberty further to express the opinion that the abnormal situation, to which you correctly refer in your message, has an unfavorable effect not only on the interests of the two states concerned, but also on the general international situation, increasing the element of disquiet, complicating the process of consolidating world peace and encouraging forces tending to disturb that peace.

In accordance with the above, I gladly accept your proposal to send to the United States a representative of the Soviet Government to discuss with you the questions of interest to our countries. The Soviet Government will be represented by Mr. M. M. Litvinoff, People's Commissar for Foreign Affairs, who will come to Washington at a time to be mutually agreed upon.

I am, my dear Mr. President,
Very sincerely yours,
MIKHAIL KALININ.

MR. FRANKLIN D. ROOSEVELT,
President of the United States of America,
Washington.

Thus, through the exchange of these simple letters, after many years the historic friendship between the people of Russia and the people of the United States was restored.

The dinner on the birthday anniversary of Woodrow Wilson on December twenty-eighth gave me opportunity once more to set forth the underlying policies of the American people in their relations with their sister nations. I said:

"Comprehension must be the soil in which shall grow all the fruits of friendship." Those words, used by President Wilson in the Mobile speech in 1913, can well serve as a statement of policy by the Government of the United States. That policy applies equally to a comprehension of our internal problems and our international relations.

Woodrow Wilson was a teacher, and when he used the word "comprehension" he meant it not in terms of the statesmen and political leaders and business executives and financial kings; he meant it rather in its application to the peoples of the world who are constantly going to school to learn simple truths in order that they and their neighbors can live their lives more safely, more happily, more fully.

In every continent and in every country Woodrow Wilson accelerated comprehension on the part of the people themselves. It is, I believe, true that the events of the past ten months have caused a greater interest in government, the problems of government, and the purposes of government than in any similar period in our history; and yet this recent interest and comprehension would have been impossible for the American people had they not had from Woodrow Wilson the original stimulus and the original understanding of which he spoke twenty years ago.

In that speech in Mobile, President Wilson first enunciated the definite statement that "the United States will never again seek one additional foot of territory by conquest." The United States accepted that declaration of policy. President Wilson went further, pointing out with special reference to our Latin-American neighbors that material interests must never be made superior to human liberty.

Nevertheless and largely as a result of the convulsion of the World War and its after effects, the complete fruition of that policy of unselfishness has not in every case been obtained. And in this we, all of us, have to share the responsibility.

I do not hesitate to say that if I had been engaged in a political campaign as a citizen of some other American republic I might have been strongly tempted to play upon the fears of my compatriots of that republic by charging the United States of North America with some form of imperialistic desire for selfish aggrandizement. As a citizen of some other republic, I might have found it difficult to believe fully in the altruism of the richest American republic. In particular, as a citizen of some other republic, I might have found it hard to approve of the occupation of the territory of other republics, even as a temporary measure.

It therefore has seemed clear to me as President that the time has come to supplement and to implement the declaration of President Wilson by the further declaration that the definite policy of the United States from now on is one opposed to armed intervention.

The maintenance of constitutional government in other nations is not a sacred obligation devolving upon the United States alone. The maintenance of law and the orderly processes of government in this hemisphere is the concern of each individual nation within its own borders first of all. It is only if and when the failure of orderly processes affects the other nations of the continent that it becomes their concern; and the point to stress is that in such an event it becomes the joint concern of a whole continent in which we are all neighbors.

It is the comprehension of that doctrine—a comprehension not by the leaders alone but by the peoples of all the American republics, that has made the conference now concluding its labors in Montevideo such a fine success. A better state of feeling among the neighbor nations of North and Central and South America exists today than at any time within a generation. For participation in the bringing about of that result we can feel proud that so much credit belongs to the Secretary of State of the United States, Cordell Hull.

In the wider world field a chain of events has led, of late, away from rather than towards the ultimate objectives of Woodrow Wilson.

The superficial observer charges this failure to the growth of the spirit of nationalism. But, in so doing he suggests a nationalism in its narrower, restrictive sense, and a nationalism of that kind supported by the overwhelming masses of the people themselves in each nation.

I challenge that description of the world population today.

The blame for the danger to world peace lies not in the world population but in the political leaders of that population.

The imagination of the masses of world population was stirred, as never before, by President Wilson's gallant appeal to them—to those masses—to banish future war. His appeal meant little to the imagination or the hearts of a large number of the so-called statesmen who gathered in Paris to assemble a treaty of so-called peace in 1919. I saw that with my own eyes and heard that with my own ears. Political profit, personal prestige, national aggrandizement attended the birth of the League of Nations, and handicapped it from its infancy by seeking their own profit and their own safety first.

Nevertheless, through the League directly, or through its guiding motives indirectly, the states of the world have groped forward to find something better than the old way of composing their differences.

The League has provided a common meeting place; it has provided machinery which serves for international discussion; and in very many practical instances it has helped labor and health and commerce and education, and last but not least, the actual settlement of many disputes great and small among nations great and small.

Today the United States is co-operating openly in the fuller utilization of the League of Nations machinery than ever before.

I believe that I express the views of my countrymen when I state that the old policies, alliances, combinations and balances of power have proved themselves inadequate for the preservation of world peace. The League of Nations, encouraging as it does the extension of nonaggression pacts, of reduction of armament agreements, is a prop in the world peace structure.

We are not members and we do not contemplate membership. We are giving co-operation to the League in every matter which is not primarily political and in every matter which obviously represents the views and the good of the peoples of the world as distinguished from the views and the good of political leaders, of privileged classes or of imperialistic aims.

If you figure the world's population at approximately one billion and a half people, you will find it safe to guess that at least 90 per cent of all of them are today content with the territorial limits of their respective nations and are willing further to reduce their armed forces tomorrow if every other nation in the world will agree to do the same thing. Back of the threat to world peace lies the fear and perhaps even the possibility that the other ten per cent of the people of the world may go along with a leadership which seeks territorial expansion at the expense of neighbors and which under various pleas in avoidance are unwilling to reduce armament or stop rearmament even if everybody else agrees to nonaggression and to arms reduction.

If this ten per cent can be persuaded by the other 90 per cent to do their own thinking and not be led, we will have practical peace, permanent peace, real peace throughout the world. Our own country has reduced the immediate steps to this greatest of objectives to practical and reasonable terms.

I have said to every nation in the world something to this effect:

1. Let every nation agree to eliminate over a short period of years, and by progressive steps, every weapon of offense in its possession and to create no additional weapons of offense. This does not guarantee a nation against invasion unless you implement it with the right to fortify its own border with permanent and nonmobile defenses; and also with the right to assure itself through international continuing inspection that its neighbors are not creating or maintaining offensive weapons of war.

2. A simple declaration that no nation will permit any of its armed forces to cross its own borders into the territory of another nation. Such an act would be regarded by humanity as an act of aggression and, as an act, therefore, that would call for condemnation by humanity.

3. It is clear, of course, that no such general agreement for the elimination of aggression and of the weapons of offensive warfare would be of any value to the world unless every nation, without exception, entered into the agreement by solemn obligation. If then such an agreement were

signed by a great majority of the nations on the definite conditions that it would go into effect only when signed by all the nations, it would be a comparatively easy matter to determine which nations in this enlightened time are willing to go on record as belonging to the small minority of mankind which still believes in the use of the sword for invasion of and attack upon their neighbors.

I did not make this suggestion until I felt assured, after a hard-headed practical survey that the temper of the overwhelming majority of all men and women in my own country as well as those who make up the world's population, subscribes to the fundamental objective I have set forth and to the practical road to that objective. The political leaders of many of these peoples interpose and will interpose argument, excuse, befogging amendment—yes, and even ridicule. But I tell them that the men and women they serve are so far in advance of that type of leadership that we could get a world accord on world peace immediately if the people of the world spoke for themselves.

Through all the centuries and down to the world conflict of 1914 to 1918, wars were made by governments. Woodrow Wilson challenged that necessity. That challenge made the people who create and who change governments think. They wondered with Woodrow Wilson whether the people themselves could not some day prevent governments from making war.

It is but an extension of the challenge of Woodrow Wilson for us to propose in this newer generation that from now on war by governments shall be changed to peace by peoples.

CHAPTER TEN

AFTER my return to Washington early in July, the executive branch of the Government was plunged into the strenuous and difficult work of setting up and welding the new machinery authorized by the Congress.

It is not within the purpose of this book to estimate the effects of the legislation, or of the immediate results of our efforts: this spring we are still in the period of evolution. Every intelligent and honest individual in the United States can form his or her opinion as time passes; it is necessary that we bear in mind only that the program as a whole is still in the process of expansion, that it is experimental in the sense that if one method does not succeed, another method will be tried, and that there are still many measures to be put forward before we can arrive at a worthwhile estimate of the completed whole.

Therefore, in this and succeeding chapters, I shall list chronologically only some of the major actions between July, 1933, and March 4, 1934.

Some of the speeches and messages, however, picture clearly the program of recovery and reorganization and outline the evolution of policy.

On July eighth, Secretary of the Interior Ickes was appointed Administrator of Public Works, and he proceeded immediately to the difficult task of allotting the vast expenditure of three billion, three hundred million dollars.

On July eleventh, I constituted the Executive Council for the simple reason that so many new agencies having been created, a weekly meeting with them and the members of the Cabinet in joint session, was imperative. At these Tuesday meetings, we had in addition to the Cabinet, the following: The Director of the Budget, the Chairman of the Board of the Reconstruction Finance Corporation, the Governor of the Farm Credit Administration, Chairman of the Board of the Home Owners' Loan Corporation, the Administor of the Agricultural Adjustment Administration, the Federal Relief Administrator, the Chairman of the Board of the Tennessee Valley Authority, the Federal Co-ordinator of Transportation, the Administrator for Industrial Recovery, and the Director of the Civilian Conservation

Corps. Mr. Frank C. Walker was appointed as Executive Secretary of the Council.

On July fourteenth, the Secretary of the Interior was also given full charge of the Oil Administration.

On July twenty-first, twenty million dollars was set aside from the public works funds for the purchase of forest lands, that additional areas might be used for the work of the Civilian Conservation Corps.

On July twenty-fourth, I reviewed over the radio the events of the previous few months as follows:

After the adjournment of the historical special session of the Congress five weeks ago I purposely refrained from addressing you for two very good reasons.

First, I think that we all wanted the opportunity of a little quiet thought to examine and assimilate in a mental picture the crowding events of the hundred days which had been devoted to the starting of the wheels of the New Deal.

Second, I wanted a few weeks in which to set up the new administrative organization and to see the first fruits of our careful planning.

I think it will interest you if I set forth the fundamentals of this planning for national recovery; and this I am very certain will make it abundantly clear to you that all of the proposals and all of the legislation since the fourth day of March have not been just a collection of haphazard schemes but rather the orderly component parts of a connected and logical whole.

Long before Inauguration Day I became convinced that individual effort and local effort and even disjointed Federal effort had failed and of necessity would fail and, therefore, that a rounded leadership by the Federal Government had become a necessity both of theory and of fact. Such leadership, however, had its beginning in preserving and strengthening the credit of the United States Government, because without that no leadership was a possibility. For years the Government had not lived within its income. The immediate task was to bring our regular expenses within our revenues. That has been done.

It may seem inconsistent for a government to cut down its regular expenses and at the same time to borrow and to spend billions for an emergency. But it is not inconsistent because a large portion of the emergency money has been paid out in the form of sound loans which will be repaid to the Treasury over a period of years; and to cover the rest of the emergency money we have imposed taxes to pay the interest and the installments on that part of the debt.

So you will see that we have kept our credit good. We have built a granite foundation in a period of confusion. That foundation of the Federal credit stands there broad and sure. It is the base of the whole recovery plan.

Then came the part of the problem that concerned the credit of the individual citizens themselves. You and I know of the banking crisis and of the great danger to the savings of our people. On March sixth every national bank was closed. One month later ninety per cent of the deposits in the national banks had been made available to the depositors. Today only about five per cent of the deposits in national banks are still tied up. The condition relating to State banks, while not quite so good on a percentage basis, is showing a steady reduction in the total of frozen deposits—a result much better than we had expected three months ago.

The problem of the credit of the individual was made more difficult because of another fact. The dollar was a different dollar from the one with which the average debt had been incurred. For this reason large numbers of people were actually losing possession of and title to their farms and homes. All of you know the financial steps which have been taken to correct this inequality. In addition the Home Loan Act, the Farm Loan Act and the Bankruptcy Act were passed.

It was a vital necessity to restore purchasing power by reducing the debt and interest charges upon our people, but while we were helping people to save their credit it was at the same time absolutely essential to do something about the physical needs of hundreds of thousands who were in dire straits at that very moment. Municipal and State aid were being stretched to the limit. We appropriated half a billion dollars to supplement their efforts and in addition, as you know, we have put 300,000 young men into practical and useful work in our forests and to prevent flood and soil erosion. The wages they earn are going in greater part to the support of the nearly one million people who constitute their families.

In this same classification we can properly place the great public works program running to a total of over three billion dollars—to be used for highways and ships and flood prevention and inland navigation and thousands of self-sustaining State and municipal improvements. Two points should be made clear in the allotting and administration of these projects—first, we are using the utmost care to choose labor-creating quick-acting, useful projects, avoiding the smell of the pork barrel; and secondly, we are hoping that at least half of the money will come back to the Government from projects which will pay for themselves over a period of years.

Thus far I have spoken primarily of the foundation stones—the measures that were necessary to re-establish credit and to head people in the opposite direction by preventing distress and providing as much work as possible through governmental agencies. Now I come to the links which will build us a more lasting prosperity. I have said that we cannot attain that in a nation half boom and half broke. If all of our people have work and fair wages and fair profits, they can buy the products of their neighbors and business is good. But if you take away the wages and the profits of half of them, business is only half as good. It doesn't help much if the fortunate half is very prosperous—the best way is for everybody to be reasonably prosperous.

For many years the two great barriers to a normal prosperity have been low farm prices and the creeping paralysis of unemployment. These factors have cut the purchasing power of the country in half. I promised action. Congress did its part when it passed the Farm and the Industrial Recovery Acts. Today we are putting these two acts to work and they will work if people understand their plain objectives.

First, the Farm Act: It is based on the fact that the purchasing power of nearly half our population depends on adequate prices for farm products. We have been producing more of some crops than we consume or can sell in a depressed world market. The cure is not to produce so much. Without our help the farmers cannot get together and cut production, and the Farm Bill gives them a method of bringing their production down to a reasonable level and of obtaining reasonable prices for their crops. I have clearly stated that this method is in a sense experimental, but so far as we have gone we have reason to believe that it will produce good results.

It is obvious that if we can greatly increase the purchasing power of the tens of millions of our people who make a living from farming and the distribution of farm crops, we will greatly increase the consumption of those goods which are turned out by industry.

That brings me to the final step—bringing back industry along sound lines.

Last autumn, on several occasions, I expressed my faith that we can make possible by democratic self-discipline in industry general increases in wages and shortening of hours sufficient to enable industry to pay its own workers enough to let those workers buy and use the things that their labor produces. This can be done only if we permit and encourage co-operative action in industry because it is obvious that without united action a few selfish men in each competitive group will pay starvation wages and insist on long hours of work. Others in that group must either follow suit or close up shop. We have seen the result of action of that kind in the continuing descent into the economic hell of the past four years.

There is a clear way to reverse that process: If all employers in each competitive group agree to pay their workers the same wages—reasonable wages—and require the same hours—reasonable hours—then higher wages and shorter hours will hurt no employer. Moreover, such action is better for the employer than unemployment and low wages, because it makes more buyers for his product. That is the simple idea which is the very heart of the Industrial Recovery Act.

On the basis of this simple principle of everybody doing things together, we are starting out on this nation-wide attack on unemployment. It will succeed if our people understand it—in the big industries, in the little shops, in the great cities and in the small villages. There is nothing complicated about it and there is nothing particularly new in the principle. It goes back to the basic idea of society and of the nation itself that people acting in a group can accomplish things which no individual acting alone could even hope to bring about.

Here is an example. In the Cotton Textile Code, and in other agreements already signed, child labor has been abolished. That makes me personally happier than any other one thing with which I have been connected since I came to Washington. In the textile industry—an industry which came to me spontaneously and with a splendid co-operation as soon as the Recovery Act was signed—child labor was an old evil. But no employer acting alone was able to wipe it out. If one employer tried it, or if one State tried it, the costs of operation rose so high that it was impossible to compete with the employers or States which had failed to act. The moment the Recovery Act was passed, this monstrous thing which neither opinion nor law could reach through years of effort went out in a flash. As a British editorial put it, we did more under a code in one day than they in England had been able to do under the common law in eighty-five years of effort. I use this incident, my friends, not to boast of what has already been done but to point the way to you for even greater co-operative efforts this summer and autumn.

We are not going through another winter like the last. I doubt if ever any people so bravely and cheerfully endured a season half so bitter. We cannot ask America to continue to face such needless hardships. It is time for courageous action, and the Recovery Bill gives us the means to conquer unemployment with exactly the same weapon that we have used to strike down child labor.

The proposition is simply this:

If all employers will act together to shorten hours and raise wages we can put people back to work. No employer will suffer, because the relative level of competitive cost will advance by the same amount for all. But if any considerable group should lag or shirk, this great opportunity will pass us by and we will go into another desperate winter. This must not happen.

We have sent out to all employers an agreement which is the result of weeks of consultation. This agreement checks against the voluntary codes of nearly all the large industries which have already been submitted. This blanket agreement carries the unanimous approval of the three boards which I have appointed to advise in this, boards representing the great leaders in labor, in industry and in social service. The agreement has already brought a flood of approval from every State, and from so wide a cross section of the common calling of industry that I know it is fair for all. It is a plan—deliberate, reasonable and just—intended to put into effect at once the most important of the broad principles which are being established, industry by industry, through codes. Naturally, it takes a good deal of organizing and a great many hearings and many months to get these codes perfected and signed, and we cannot wait for all of them to go through. The blanket agreements, however, which I am sending to every employer, will start the wheels turning now and not six months from now.

There are, of course, men, a few of them, who might thwart this great common purpose by seeking selfish advantage. There are adequate penalties in the law, but I am now asking the co-operation that comes from opinion and from conscience. These are the only instruments we shall use in this great summer offensive against unemployment. But we shall use them to the limit to protect the willing from the laggard and to make the plan succeed.

In war, in the gloom of night attack, soldiers wear a bright badge on their shoulders to be sure that comrades do not fire on comrades. On that principle, those who co-operate in this program must know each other at a glance. That is why we have provided a badge of honor for this purpose, a simple design with a legend, "We Do Our Part," and I ask that all those who join with me shall display that badge prominently. It is essential to our purpose.

Already all the great, basic industries have come forward willingly with proposed codes, and in these codes they accept the principles leading to mass re-employment. But, important as is this heartening demonstration, the richest field for results is among the small employers, those whose contribution will be to give new work for from one to ten people. These smaller employers are indeed a vital part of the backbone of the country, and the success of our plans lies largely in their hands.

Already the telegrams and letters are pouring into the White House—messages from employers who ask that their names be placed on this special Roll of Honor. They represent great corporations and companies and partnerships and individuals. I ask that even before the dates set in the agreements which we have sent out the employers of the country who have not already done so—the big fellows and the little fellows—shall at once write or telegraph to me personally at the White House, expressing their intention of going through with the plan. And it is my purpose to keep posted in the post office of every town, a Roll of Honor of all those who join with me.

I want to take this occasion to say to the twenty-four Governors who are now in conference in San Francisco, that nothing thus far has helped in strengthening this great movement more than their resolutions adopted at the very outset of their meeting, giving this plan their instant and unanimous approval, and pledging to support it in their States.

To the men and women whose lives have been darkened by the fact or the fear of unemployment, I am justified in saying a word of encouragement because the codes and the agreements already approved, or about to be passed upon, prove that the plan does raise wages, and that it does put people back to work. You can look on every employer who adopts the plan as one who is doing his part, and those employers deserve well of everyone who works for a living. It will be clear to you, as it is to me, that while the shirking employer may undersell his competitor, the saving he thus makes is made at the expense of his country's welfare.

While we are making this great common effort there should be no discord and dispute. This is no time to cavil or to question the standard set by this universal agreement. It is time for patience and understanding and co-operation. The workers of this country have rights under this law which cannot be taken from them, and nobody will be permitted to whittle them away but, on the other hand, no aggression is now necessary to attain those rights. The whole country will be united to get them for you. The principle that applies to the employers applies to the workers as well, and I ask you workers to co-operate in the same spirit.

When Andrew Jackson, "Old Hickory," died, someone asked, "Will he go to heaven," and the answer was, "He will if he wants to." If I am asked whether the American people will pull themselves out of this depression, I answer, "They will if they want to." The essence of the plan is a universal limitation of hours of work per week for any individual by common consent, and a universal payment of wages above the minimum, also by common consent. I cannot guarantee the success of this nation-wide plan, but the people of this country can guarantee its success. I have no faith in "cure-alls" but I believe that we can greatly influence economic forces. I have no sympathy with the professional economists who insist that things must run their course and that human agencies can have no influence on economic ills.

One reason is that I happen to know that professional economists have changed ther definition of economic laws every five or ten years for a very long time, but I do have faith, and retain faith, in the strength of common purpose and in the strength of unified action taken by the American people.

That is why I am describing to you the simple purposes and the solid foundations upon which our program of recovery is built. That is why I am asking the employers of the Nation to sign this common covenant with me—to sign it in the name of patriotism and humanity. That is why I am asking the workers to go along with us in a spirit of understanding and of helpfulness.

By early August the establishment of codes for industry had proceeded so far under the direction of the Administrator for Industrial Recovery, that on the unanimous recommendation of the labor and industrial leaders on the Advisory Boards of the Recovery Administration, I created by Executive Order a tribunal to be known as the National Labor Board and with the following membership: Senator Robert F. Wagner, Chairman, Mr. William Green, Dr. Leo Wolman, Mr. John L. Lewis, Mr. Walter C. Teagle, Mr. Gerard Swope and Mr. Louis E. Kirstein.

Later in the month, on August twenty-sixth, while spending two weeks at home, my neighbors of Dutchess County, N. Y., gave a home-coming reception at Vassar College. I am inserting the informal speech on that occasion because it discusses a number of fundamentals connected with our national life:

It is, I think, just twenty-three years ago that I chanced to be in Poughkeepsie on a Saturday morning in August. In front of the Court House I was kidnaped—kidnaped by Judge Morschauser, George Spratt, John Mack and Judge Arnold, and taken to the Policemen's Picnic at Fairview. On that joyous occasion of clams and sauerkraut and beer I made my first speech. And on that same occasion I started to make the acquaintance of the Dutchess County that lay outside of the Town of Hyde Park.

Through all these succeeding years the friendships then begun have deepened and in spite of the absences in Washington and in Albany I come back to the county on every possible occasion with the true feeling that it is home and that I am once more among my neighbors.

During these recent months I have taken deep satisfaction in the fine spirit of understanding with which the people of my home county have gone along with the great national effort to set our national house in order. In former days we have seen something of the same purpose in the fields of local government. Here and there a town or a city or a county or even a State has, through its citizenship, become conscious of the fact that under the old order the social, the economic or the political life of the unit was drifting down hill through lack of action or because of adherence to old rules which had been promulgated to fit conditions of a bygone age. In such individual cases aroused citizens have chosen new servants or have changed the form of conducting their local affairs to the advantage of the community without destroying the principles of self-government. History gives us many local examples in almost every State of the Union.

In a sense this arousing is what has occurred in Washington in 1933. It is the first time in our history that the Nation as a whole and regardless of party has approved drastic changes in the methods and forms of the functions of government without destroying the basic principles.

Perhaps I can best illustrate the change by telling you that we have been extending to our national life the old principle of home community —that no individual, no family, has a right to do things which hurt the neighbors. Many centuries ago that was a tenet of the old English common law and its development has been constant and consistent. It is unfair to our neighbors if we allow our cattle to roam on their land. It is unfair to our neighbors if we maintain a pigsty on Main Street. It became unfair to our neighbors if we sought to make unreasonable profit from a monopoly in a service such as electricity or gas or railroad tickets which they had to use. It became unfair to our neighbors if we tried to hire their children at starvation wages and long hours of work.

Many years ago we went even further in saying that the Government would place increasing taxes on increasing profits because very large profits were, of course, made at the expense of the neighbors and should, to some extent at least, be used for the benefit of the neighbors.

The extension of the idea of not hurting the neighbors is recognized today as no infringement on the guarantee of personal liberty to the individual because, for example, it is no more a restriction to tell a man that he must pay adequate wages than it is to tell a man that he cannot hire child labor, or that he cannot maintain a nuisance.

It is with this understanding of the deeper purposes of the National Recovery Act that the Nation is accepting its provisions and its agreements with such whole-hearted approval.

It is true, of course, that your Government hopes that the building up of wages that are starvation wages, and the shortening of hours of work in every part of the United States, will result in a greater distribution of wages and an increase in the number of persons employed. It is true that we seek definitely to increase the purchasing power of the American people. It is true

that we are definitely succeeding in this purpose and that the downhill drift has definitely turned and become an upward surge.

But it is also true that the people, through government, are extending as a permanent part of American life their insistence that individuals and associations of individuals shall cease doing many things which have been hurting their neighbors.

We are engaged in reviewing all kinds of human relationships and in these reviews we are asking a new question, "Is this practice or custom something which is being done at the expense of the many?" The many are the neighbors.

In a national sense the many, the neighbors, are the people of the United States as a whole. Nationally we must think of them as a whole and not by sections or States alone. We cannot give special consideration to the people of the North if in so doing it will not result in good to the people of the South or the West. We cannot give special privileges to those who farm one particular crop if the giving makes things more difficult for those who farm some other crop. We cannot single out one industry at the expense of others. The national Government must think in national terms.

But your responsibility for and your interest in national Government should not stop there. The greater part of government as it affects your daily lives is your local government and the opportunity in this field is at least as great as it is in Washington. As Governor I have often told you of the 13,000 units of local government, which you have in this State alone. You were interested but you did nothing. I have told you of the 950 highway departments in the State of New York. You were interested but you did nothing. I have told you of the six or eight or ten layers of government under which you live in your home. You have done nothing to reorganize what you all know to be an outworn system, built up in the days of the ox cart and unchanged in the days of the automobile. Some day the people of the State of New York will do something about it but I tell you quite frankly that nothing will be done unless you make your representatives in town boards and county boards and the State legislature do it, or substitute other representatives for them.

Again I tell you how happy I have been in the understanding of our national problems and national programs which the people have had everywhere. More men and women are taking an individual and personal interest in government and all the problems that relate thereto than ever before in the history of the Nation. I hope that that interest will be extended to the problems of local government. The old principle of the good of our neighbors holds true there, too. And it seems to me very fitting that I should emphasize to you, my neighbors of my own home county, that thought, that what is good for my neighbors is good for me, too.

With my family I am grateful to have this opportunity of seeing all our friends of old Dutchess here today. Bless you all.

I cannot refrain from mentioning that soon after our return to Washington we were greatly saddened by the death of an associate and old friend, Ike Hoover, the Chief Usher at the White House. Mrs. Roosevelt and I had known him since the Administration of President Theodore Roosevelt and the affection of those days lived through later years. It was Ike Hoover who met us when we came to the White House on March 4, 1933, who welcomed us and made us feel that we were at home. Serving in ten administrations with discretion and ability, Ike Hoover will always stand out as a true and faithful public servant and as a friend whom we deeply miss.

On October first, I went to Chicago to see the Century of Progress Exposition and to speak at the American Legion Convention. That speech, which I believe lays down certain honorable and fair principles, follows:

I am glad to come here as your guest and I am glad to have the right to come here as your comrade. I have come because I have faith in the American Legion and in all other veterans of our wars. The right which I have to come here works both ways, because as long as I am in the White House you have the right to come and see me there.

But my relationship with you is not a matter of the past six months; it dates back to the war days when I participated with you, not only in this country but also on the North Sea, and in the Channel, and on the actual fighting front in France.

I want to talk with you about the problem of government, the difficulties which you and I as Americans have faced and solved, and those which we still face. I recognize and appreciate, and the Nation recognizes and appreciates, the patience, the loyalty and the willingness to make sacrifices, shown by the overwhelming majority of the veterans of our country during the trying period from which we are beginning successfully to emerge.

I want to talk to you about national unity. Let us look at it as a living thing—not a mere theory resting in books, or otherwise apart from everyday business of men. It means that we all live under a common government, trade with each other, pay common taxes, give to and receive from a common protective government. To recognize national unity, to hold it above all else, seeing that upon it depends our common welfare, is just another way to say that we have patriotism.

You and I who served in the World War know that we represented a united nation in a time of danger to world civilization. But you and I know also that national unity is as essential in time of peace as in time of war. If this country is worth living in, if this flag of ours is worth living under, if our social order means anything to us, then this country of ours is worth defending every day and every year of the life of every individual one of us. It is because I am willing to live myself, or to have my children or grandchildren live, under an alien flag or an alien form of government, that I believe in the fundamental obligation of citizenship to don the uniform of our country, to carry arms in its defense when our country and the things it stands for are attacked.

But there are two enemies of national unity, sectionalism and class, and if the spirit of sectionalism or the spirit of class is allowed to grow strong or to prevail, it means the end of national unity and the end of patriotism.

Some people who visit us from other lands still find it difficult to credit the fact that a nation sprung from many sources, a nation one hundred and thirty million strong, a nation stretching three thousand miles from east to west, is, in all the great essentials of its civilization, a homogeneous whole; for not only do we speak one language, not only are the customs and habits of our people similar in every part of the continent, but we have given repeated proof on many occasions, and especially in recent years, that we are willing to forego sectional advantage where such advantage can be obtained only by one part of the country at the expense of another.

The other enemy of national unity is class distinction, and you and I are well aware of the simple fact that as every day passes, the people of this country are less and less willing to tolerate benefits for any one group of citizens which must be paid for by others.

You have been willing to fight for the benefits of American life. You have been willing to live for American unity. You have understood that this is the very foundation of the Americanism for which you stand, in which you believe, and to which you and I swore allegiance when we became American Legionnaires.

For several years past the benefits of American life were threatened. The crisis came in the spring of this year. It was necessary to meet that crisis. Again it was necessary for all of us to go back to fundamentals. Millions were out of work, the banks were closed, the credit of the Government itself was threatened. The car was stalled. Obviously, the first objective was to get the engine running again. It is true that we succeeded in reopening the great majority of the banks, but this would not have been possible if at the same time we had not been able to restore the credit of the Government.

In speaking of national credit we are again dealing with a real thing, not a theory in books. There is such a thing as national credit. It depends upon national unity. Without it the Government cannot get the money to give. You and I depend upon it, and in a right sense your welfare and mine rests upon it.

That is not just an academic proposition. Industry cannot be restored, people cannot be put back to work, banks cannot be kept open, human suffering cannot be cared for, if the Government itself is bankrupt. We realize now that the great human values, not for you alone but for all American citizens, rest upon the unimpaired credit of the United States.

It was because of this that we undertook to take the National Treasury out of the red and put it into the black. And in the doing of it we laid down two principles which directly affected benefits to veterans—to you, and to veterans of other wars.

The first principle, following inevitably from the obligation of citizens to bear arms, is that the Government has a responsibility for and towards those who suffered injury or contracted disease while serving in its defense.

The second principle is that no person because he wore a uniform must thereafter be placed in a special class of beneficiaries over and above all other citizens. The fact of wearing a uniform does not mean that he can demand and receive from his Government a benefit which no other citizen

164

receives. It does not mean that because a person served in the defense of his country, performed a basic obligation of citizenship, he should receive a pension from his Government because of a disability incurred after his service had terminated and not connected with that service.

It does mean, however, that those who were injured in or as a result of their service, are entitled to receive adequate and generous compensation for their disabilities. It does mean that generous care shall be extended to the dependents of those who died in or as a result of service to their country.

To carry out these principles, the people of this country can and will pay in taxes the sums which it is necessary to raise. To carry out these principles will not bankrupt your Government nor throw its bookkeeping into the red.

Every person who has made honest study knows that mistakes, many of them, have been made during the course of fifteen years. I personally know that mistakes in individual cases and inequalities affecting various groups have occurred during the past six months. But at the same time there stands out the fact which you know—that many of these mistakes have been rectified and that we have the definite purpose of doing justice not only to the mass, but, in so far as possible, to every individual as well. Furthermore, it is my hope that in so far as justice concerns those whose disabilities are, as a matter of fact, of war service origin, the Government will be able to extend even more generous care than is now provided under existing regulations. It is to these men that our obligation exists.

To these two broad principles the time has come, I believe, for us to add a third. There are many veterans of our wars to whom disability and sickness unconnected with war service has come. To them the Federal Government owes the application of the same rule which it has laid down for the relief of other cases of involuntary want or destitution.

In other words, if the individual affected can afford to pay for his own treatment he cannot call on any form of government aid. If he has not the wherewithal to take care of himself, it is first of all the duty of his community to take care of him and next the duty of his State. Only if under these circumstances his own community and his own State are unable, after reasonable effort, to care for him, then, and then only, should the Federal Government offer him hospitalization and care.

The young men of this country who today, in the event of war, would bear the first brunt of national defense, think of us of the American Legion as middle-aged people. You and I are not yet ready to admit that we have "one foot in the grave." We think of ourselves and with some justification perhaps, as people of some experience, of some maturity of judgment, of a position in the community which carries responsibilities. We believe we have influence as individuals and we believe that as an organization the American Legion has enormous power for the good of the country for many years to come. It is not enough that you have helped to write the history of America. It is a fact that much of the future history of America will be a history which you will help to make. Your future interests are inseparable from those of our citizens, and, granting that your interest in the disabled and dependent comrades is first upon your program, I ask in addition your co-operation in the great program of national rehabilitation in which you and I are equally engaged.

The charter of the Legion keeps it out of partisan politics. The strength and the very existence of the Legion depend on the maintenance of that principle. You are not here as Republicans or Democrats. You are here, as you should be, as Americans to work with your Government for the good of the average citizen. I am grateful to the Legion for the splendid stand it has taken—for the "Battle Order" it has issued.

The realization of our national program cannot be attained in six months. Re-employment has proceeded only a part of the way. From week to week there will be ups and downs, but the net result is a consistent gain. The freezing of credits has been stopped and the ice is definitely melting. Farm income has been increased; it must be further increased. Industry has picked up, but an increased purchasing power must stimulate it further.

Your task and mine are similar. Each one of us must play an individual part in our own field in dealing with these many problems but at the same time we must realize that the individual parts belong to a closely related whole—the national unity of purpose and of action.

I ask your further and even greater efforts in our program of national recovery. You who wore the uniform, you who served, you who took the oath of allegiance to the American Legion, you who support the ideals of American citizenship, I have called to the Colors again. As your Commander-in-Chief and your comrade, I am confident that you will respond.

On October fourth, I spoke in New York at the dinner of the National Conference of Catholic Charities:

In the midst of problems of material things—in the machine age of invention, of finance, of international suspicion and renewed armament—every one of us must gain satisfaction and strength in the knowledge that social justice is becoming an ever-growing factor and influence in almost every part of the world. With every passing year I become more confident that humanity is moving forward to the practical application of the teachings of Christianity as they affect the individual lives of men and women.

It is fitting that this annual National Conference of Catholic Charities should celebrate also the centennial of the Society of St. Vincent de Paul. I like to remember the taunt of atheists and enemies of the Christian religion in the Paris of 1833, when they demanded of the churches, "Show us your works." I like to think of the acceptance of that challenge and the decision to show that Christianity was not dead, and that the deeds of Christians were in accordance with their faith. When I realize that this one society, last year, in its task of visitation and relief of the poor in their own homes, in hospitals and institutions, aided more than one hundred and fifty thousand families; and that other great organizations of men and women connected with all the churches in all the land are working with similar unselfishness for the alleviation of human suffering and the righting of human wrong, I am confirmed in my deep belief that God is marching on.

Seven months ago this very day, standing at the portals of the Capitol at Washington, about to assume the responsibilities of the presidency, I told the people of America that we were going to face facts, no matter how hard or difficult those facts might be, and that it was my firm belief that the only thing we had to fear was fear itself.

I believed then—and I know now—that our people would support definite action that sought the goal of giving every man his due. Leadership, I have tried to give; but the great and most important fact has been the response—the whole-hearted response—of America. We have recaptured and rekindled our pioneering spirit. We have insisted that this shall always be a spirit of justice, a spirit of teamwork, a spirit of sacrifice, and, above all, a spirit of neighborliness.

We have sought to adjust the processes of industrial and agricultural life, and in so doing we have sought to view the picture as a whole. Revival of industry, redemption of agriculture, reconstruction of banking, development of public works, the lifting of crushing debt—all these in every part of the Nation call for a willingness to sacrifice individual gains, to work together for the public welfare and for the success of a broad national program of recovery. We have to have courage and discipline and vision to blaze the new trails in life; but underlying all our efforts is the conviction that men cannot live unto themselves alone. A democracy must be bound together by the ties of neighborliness.

That tie has been the guiding spirit of your work for the sick, for the children in need, and for the aged and friendless. And you who have participated in the actual day-to-day work of practical and useful charity understand well that no program of recovery can suddenly restore all our people to self-support. This is the time when you and I know that though we have proceeded a portion of the way, the longer, harder part still lies ahead; and that it is for us to redouble our efforts to care for those who must still depend upon relief, to prevent the disintegration of home life, and to stand by the victims of the depression until it is definitely past.

The Federal Government has inaugurated new measures of relief on a vast scale, but the Federal Government cannot, and does not intend, to take over the whole job. Many times I have insisted that every community and every State must first do its share.

Out of this picture we are developing a new science of social treatment and rehabilitation—working it out through an unselfish partnership between all church and private social service agencies with the agencies of Government itself. From the point of view of the fixing of responsibilities, the prevention of overlapping and of waste, and the co-ordination of efforts, we are making enormous strides with every passing day. But back of the co-operative leadership which is showing itself in every part of the country, there are two other vital reasons for the maintenance of the efforts of the churches and other non-governmental groups.

The first of these is that much as we strive for the broad principles of social justice, the actual application of these principles is of necessity an individual thing—a thing which touches individual lives and individual families. No governmental organization in all history has been able to keep the human touch to the same extent as church and private effort. Government can do many things better than private associations or citizens, but in the last analysis success in personal matters depends on the personal contact between neighbor and neighbor.

The other reason lies in the fact that the people of the United States still recognize, and, I believe, recognize with firmer faith than ever before, that spiritual values count in the long run more than material values. Those who have sought by edict to eliminate the right of mankind to believe in God and to practice that belief, have, in every case, discovered sooner or later that they are tilting in vain against an inherent, essential, undying quality, and indeed necessity, of the human race—a quality and a necessity which in every century have proved an essential to permanent progress.

Clear thinking and earnest effort and sincere faith will result in thoroughgoing support throughout the whole Nation for efforts such as yours. The spirit of our people has not been daunted. It has come through the trials of those days unafraid. We have ventured and we have won; we shall venture further and we shall win. The traditions of a great people have been enriched. In our measure of recovery and of relief we have preserved all that is best in our history and are building thereon a new structure—strong and firm and permanent.

I can never express in words what the loyalty and trust of the Nation have meant to me. Not for a moment have I doubted that we would climb out of the valley of gloom. Always have I been certain that we could conquer, because the spirit of America springs from faith—faith in the beloved institutions of our land, and a true and abiding faith in the divine guidance of God.

In October, we created a Deposit Liquidation Board to expedite the payment of deposits in banks which had previously closed and were not in condition to reopen. At the same time, the Reconstruction Finance Corporation, working with the Controller of the Currency and the Federal Reserve System, undertook through the purchase of preferred stock to restore the capital of many banks in order that they might qualify under the deposit insurance plan which was to go into effect on January first.

For the fourth time during the year, I reviewed the national situation on the radio. This speech of October twenty-second announced for the first time the policy of the Government to purchase newly mined gold in the United States, and also to buy or sell gold in the world market:

It is three months since I have talked with the people of this country about our national problems; but during this period many things have happened, and I am glad to say that the major part of them have greatly helped the well-being of the average citizen.

Because, in every step which your Government is taking we are thinking in terms of the average of you—in the old words "the greatest good to the greatest number"—we, as reasonable people, cannot expect to bring definite benefits to every person or to every occupation or business, or industry or agriculture. In the same way no reasonable person can expect that in this short space of time, during which new machinery had to be not only put to work, but first set up, that every locality in every one of the 48 States of the country, could share equally and simultaneously in the trend to better times.

The whole picture, however—the average of the whole territory from coast to coast—the average of the whole population of 120,000,000 people—shows to any person willing to look facts and action of which you and I can be proud.

In the early spring of this year there were actually and proportionately more people out of work in this country than in any other nation in the world. Fair estimates showed 12 or 13 millions unemployed last March. Among those there were, of course, several millions who could be classed as normally unemployed—people who worked

174

occasionally when they felt like it, and others who preferred not to work at all. It seems, therefore, fair to say that there were about ten millions of our citizens who earnestly, and in many cases hungrily, were seeking work and could not get it. Of these, in the short space of a few months, I am convinced that at least four millions have been given employment—or, saying it another way, 40 per cent of those seeking work have found it.

That does not mean, my friends, that I am satisfied, or that you are satisfied that our work is ended. We have a long way to go but we are on the way.

How are we constructing the edifice of recovery —the temple which, when completed, will no longer be a temple of money changers or of beggars but rather a temple dedicated to and maintained for a greater social justice, a greater welfare for America—the habitation of a sound economic life. We are building, stone by stone, the columns which will support that habitation. Those columns are many in number and though, for a moment the progress of one column may disturb the progress on the pillar next to it, the work on all of them must proceed without let or hindrance.

We all know that immediate relief for the unemployed was the first essential of such a structure and that is why I speak first of the fact that three hundred thousand young men have been given employment and are being given employment all through this winter in the Civilian Conservation Corps camps in almost every part of the Nation.

So, too, we have, as you know, expended greater sums in co-operation with States and localities for work relief and home relief than ever before—sums which during the coming winter cannot be lessened for the very simple reason that though several million people have gone back to work, the necessities of those who have not yet obtained work is more severe than at this time last year.

Then we come to the relief that is being given to those who are in danger of losing their farms or their homes. New machinery had to be set up for farm credit and for home credit in every one of the thirty-one hundred counties of the United States and every day that passes is saving homes and farms to hundreds of families. I have publicly asked that foreclosures on farms and chattels and on homes be delayed until every mortgagor in the country shall have had full opportunity to take advantage of Federal credit. I make the further request, which many of you know has already been made through the great Federal credit organizations, that if there is any family in the United States about to lose its home or about to lose its chattels, that family should telegraph at once either to the Farm Credit Administration or the Home Owners Loan Corporation in Washington requesting their help.

Two other great agencies are in full swing. The Reconstruction Finance Corporation continues to lend large sums to industry and finance with the definite objective of making easy the extending of credit to industry, commerce and finance.

The program of public works in three months has advanced to this point: Out of a total appropriated for public works of three billion three hundred million, one billion eight hundred million has already been allocated to Federal projects of all kinds, and literally in every part of the United States, and work on these is starting forward. In addition three hundred millions have been allocated to public works to be carried out by States, municipalities and private organizations, such as those undertaking slum clearance. The balance of the public works money, nearly all of it intended for State or local projects, waits only on the presentation of proper projects by the States and localities themselves. Washington has the money and is waiting for the proper projects to which to allot it.

Another pillar in the making is the Agricultural Adjustment Administration. I have been amazed by the extraordinary degree of co-operation given to the Government by the cotton farmers of the South, the wheat farmers of the West, the tobacco farmers of the Southeast, and I am confident that the corn hog farmers of the Middle West will come through in the same magnificent fashion. The problem we seek to solve had been steadily getting worse for twenty years but during the last six months we have made more rapid progress than any nation has ever made in a like period of time. It is true that in July farm commodity prices had been pushed up higher than they are today, but that push came in part from pure speculation by people who could not tell you the difference between wheat and rye, by people who had never seen cotton growing, by people who did not know that hogs were fed on corn—people who have no real interest in the farmer and his problems.

In spite, however, of the speculative reaction from the speculative advance, it seems to be well established that during the course of the year 1933 the farmers of the United States will receive 33 per cent more dollars for what they have produced than they received in the year 1932. Put in another way, they will receive $400 in 1933, where they received $300 the year before. That, remember, is for the average of the country, for I have reports that some sections are not any better off than they were a year ago. This applies among the major products, especially to cattle raising and dairy industry. We are going after those problems as fast as we can.

I do not hesitate to say in the simplest, clearest language of which I am capable, that although the prices of many products of the farm have gone up and although many farm families are better off than they were last year, I am not satisfied either with the amount or the extent of the rise, and that it is definitely a part of our policy to increase the rise and to extend it to those products which have as yet felt no benefit. If we cannot do this one way we will do it another. Do it, we will.

Standing beside the pillar of the farm—the AAA —is the pillar of industry—the NRA. Its object is to put industry and business workers into employment and to increase their purchasing power through increased wages.

It has abolished child labor. It has eliminated the sweat shop. It has ended sixty cents a week paid in some mills and eighty cents a week paid in some mines. The measure of the growth of this pillar lies in the total figures of re-employment which I have already given you and in the fact that re-employment is continuing and not stopping. The secret of NRA is co-operation. That co-operation has been voluntarily given through the signing of the blanket codes and through the signing of specific codes which already include all of the greater industries of the nation.

In the vast majority of cases, in the vast majority of localities, the NRA has been given support in unstinted measure. We know that there are chisellers. At the bottom of every case of criticism and obstruction we have found some selfish interest, some private axe to grind.

Ninety per cent of complaints come from misconception. For example, it has been said that NRA has failed to raise the price of wheat and corn and hogs; that NRA has not loaned enough money for local public works. Of course, NRA has nothing whatsoever to do with the price of farm products, nor with public works. It has to do only with industrial organization for economic planning, to wipe out unfair practices and to create re-employment. Even in the field of business and industry NRA does not apply to the rural communities or to towns of under twenty-five hundred population, except in so far as those towns contain factories or chain stores which come under a specific code.

It is also true that among the chisellers to whom I have referred, there are not only the big chisellers but also petty chisellers who seek to make undue profit on untrue statements.

Let me cite to you the example of the salesman in a store in a large eastern city who tried to justify the increase in the price of a cotton shirt from one dollar and a half to two dollars and a half by saying to the customer that it was due to the cotton processing tax. Actually in that shirt there was about one pound of cotton and the processing tax amounted to four and a quarter cents on that pound of cotton.

At this point it is only fair that I should give credit to the sixty or seventy million people who live in the cities and larger towns of the Nation for their understanding and their willingness to go along with the payment of even these small processing taxes, though they know full well that the proportion of the processing taxes on cotton goods and on food products paid for by city dwellers goes one hundred per cent towards increasing the agricultural income of the farm dwellers of the land.

The last pillar of which I speak is that of the money of the country in the banks of the country. There are two simple facts.

First, the Federal Government is about to spend one billion dollars as an immediate loan on the frozen or non-liquid assets of all banks closed since January 1, 1933, giving a liberal appraisal to those assets. This money will be in the hands of the depositors as quickly as it is humanly possible to get it out.

Second, the Government Bank Deposit Insurance on all accounts up to $2,500 goes into effect on January first. We are now engaged in seeing to it that on or before that date the banking capital structure will be built up by the Government to the point that the banks will be in sound condition when the insurance goes into effect.

Finally, I repeat what I have said on many occasions, that ever since last March the definite policy of the Government has been to restore commodity price levels. The object has been the attainment of such a level as will enable agriculture and industry once more to give work to the unemployed. It has been to make possible the payment of public and private debts more nearly at the price level at which they were incurred. It has been gradually to restore a balance in the price structure so that farmers may exchange their products for the products of industry on a fairer exchange basis. It has been and is also the purpose to prevent prices from rising beyond the point necessary to attain these ends. The permanent welfare and security of every class of our people ultimately depends on our attainment of these purposes.

Obviously, and because hundreds of different kinds of crops and industrial occupations in the huge territory that makes up this Nation are involved, we cannot reach the goal in only a few months. We may take one year or two years or three years.

No one who considers the plain facts of our situation believes that commodity prices, especially agricultural prices, are high enough yet.

Some people are putting the cart before the horse. They want a permanent revaluation of the dollar first. It is the Government's policy to restore the price level first. I would not know, and no one else could tell, just what the permanent valuation of the dollar will be. To guess at a permanent gold valuation now would certainly require later changes caused by later facts.

When we have restored the price level, we shall seek to establish and maintain a dollar which will not change its purchasing and debt-paying power during the succeeding generation. I said that in my message to the American delegation in London last July. And I say it now once more.

Because of conditions in this country and because of events beyond our control in other parts of the world, it becomes increasingly important to develop and apply the further measures which may be necessary from time to time to control the gold value of our own dollar at home.

Our dollar is now altogether too greatly influenced by the accidents of international trade, by the internal policies of other nations and by political disturbance in other continents. Therefore the United States must take firmly in its own hands the control of the gold value of our dollar. This is necessary in order to prevent dollar disturbances from swinging us away from our ultimate goal, namely, the continued recovery of our commodity prices.

As a further effective means to this end, I am going to establish a government market for gold in the United States. Therefore, under the clearly defined authority of existing law, I am authorizing the Reconstruction Finance Corporation to buy gold newly mined in the United States at prices to be determined from time to time after consultation with the Secretary of the Treasury and the President. Whenever necessary to the end in view, we shall also buy or sell gold in the world market.

My aim in taking this step is to establish and maintain continuous control.

This is a policy and not an expedient.

It is not to be used merely to offset a temporary fall in prices. We are thus continuing to move toward a managed currency.

You will recall the dire predictions made last spring by those who did not agree with our common policies of raising prices by direct means. What actually happened stood out in sharp contrast with those predictions. Government credit is high, prices have risen in part. Doubtless prophets of evil still exist in our midst. But government credit will be maintained and a sound currency will accompany a rise in the American commodity price level.

I have told you tonight the story of our steady but sure work in building our common recovery. In my promsies to you, both before and after March fourth, I made two things plain: First, that I pledged no miracles, and, second, that I would do my best.

I thank you for your patience and your faith. Our troubles will not be over tomorrow, but we are on our way and we are headed in the right direction.

In spite of every effort, re-employment up to this time had not progressed as fast as we had hoped. We were faced by the coming of winter with many million people still on relief rolls. By the transfer of four hundred million dollars from the Public Works Administration, we set up the Civil Works Administration under Mr. Hopkins. This statement, made on November eighth, shows the purpose of, and the need for, this decision which did so much to carry the United States successfully through the difficult winter of 1933-34:

Four million men now out of employment will be put to work under a plan announced today by the President.

Two million of these will become self-sustaining employees on Federal, State and local public projects on November sixteenth, and will be taken completely off the relief rolls. An additional two million will be put back to work as soon thereafter as possible.

This plan will be administered by the newly created Civil Works Administration. The President today appointed Mr. Harry L. Hopkins as Administrator.

The Civil Works Administration will be financed jointly by funds from the Public Works Administration and the Federal Emergency Relief Administration, but States, cities, counties and towns will be required to provide the funds to meet their share of the Civil Works program.

Secretary Harold L. Ickes, Public Works Administrator, was prepared to make available an amount up to $400,000,000 to the Civil Works Administration.

The two million men comprise those now on work relief provided by local relief administrations operating under the State and Federal emergency relief administrations. These will immediately be placed on regular pay at the hourly rates prevailing for similar work in the community. The program contemplates a 30-hour week for the workers.

Work relief divisions of the existing State and local emergency unemployment relief administrations will be modified to perform the expanded employment activities and will be known as Civil Works Divisions.

Creation of the new agency constitutes a fundamental change in the Federal program to deal with unemployment aspects of the depression. It will remove from the relief rolls a major portion of those receiving the necessities of life on the basis of public aid and place them on regular employment. It is designed to remove from relief all employable persons. Those hired by the Civil Works Administration will benefit by an immediate increase in income over their former relief allowances.

The projects on which the workers will be used will include not only the type on which work-relief is now being given, but also a wide range of employment in activities bordering on but not covered in the province of the Public Works Administration. This expanded field will enable the local Civil Works Divisions to undertake considerably more construction and to use greater quantities of construction materials. Work relief has been limited almost entirely to work involving a minimum of materials, since expenditure of emergency relief funds under this method was necessarily confined to relief allowances in the form of work-relief wages.

Approximately 3,000,000 families are now being cared for throughout the country by public relief administrations financed in whole or part by Federal emergency relief funds.

Approximately 2,000,000 adult members of these families are earning relief in the form of wages for part-time employment on made-work projects. The total amount earned by the members of any one family is less than $20 a month in most localities.

By this one stroke at least two-thirds of the families in the country now receiving relief will be placed on a self-sustaining basis.

On November seventeenth, I left for a two weeks' holiday at Warm Springs, stopping in Savannah the next day to attend the celebration of the Bicentennial of the founding of Georgia. I said on this occasion:

Because my other State gave me the privilege of serving as the Honorary Chairman of the Celebration of this Bicentennial year of the founding of Georgia I have come to Savannah in an official capacity.

But I come here also because of all that Georgia

means to me personally, through my long association with this State and also through the kinship which my wife and my children bear to the early settlers who participated with Oglethorpe in the founding of civilization on this portion of the Atlantic Seaboard.

Apart from the ties of Colonial ancestry, I have additional kinship with the founders of the thirteen American colonies. It has been remarked of late by certain modern Tories that those who are today in charge of your National Government are guilty of great experimentation. If I read my history right, the same suggestion was used when Englishmen, protesting in vain against intolerable conditions at home, founded new colonies in the American wilderness, and when Washingtons and Adamses and Bullochs conducted another great experiment in 1776.

Three-quarters of a year have passed since I left Georgia; during that time you have conducted a dignified and history-teaching, statewide celebration. During that same time, the lives of the people of this commonwealth, like the lives of the inhabitants of the other States, have undergone a great change.

I am happy in the thought that it has been a change for the better; that I come back to see smiles replacing gloom, to see hope replacing despair, to see faith restored to its rightful place.

While we are celebrating the planting of the Colony of Georgia, we remember that if the early settlers had been content to remain on the coast, there would have been no Georgia today. It was the spirit of moving forward that led to the exploration of the great domain of piedmont and mountains that drove the western border of the colony to the very banks of the Mississippi River itself. In all those years of the pioneer, there were the doubting Thomases, there was the persistent opposition of those who feared change, of those who played the part of the mule who had to be goaded to get him out of the stable.

In coming for a two weeks' visit among you my neighbors, I shall have opportunity to improve myself by reading of the makers of our history with the thought before me that although problems and terms change, the principles and objectives of American self-government remain the same. I have heard so much of so-called economics in recent weeks that it was refreshing the other day to have my friend, the Governor of New Hampshire, call my attention to a paragraph written a century ago by that father of economists, John Stuart Mill. He said:

"History shows that great economic and social forces flow like a tide over communities only half conscious of that which is befalling them. Wise statesmen foresee what time is thus bringing and try to shape institutions and mold men's thoughts and purposes in accordance with the change that is silently coming on.

"The unwise are those who bring nothing constructive to the process, and who greatly imperil the future of mankind, by leaving great questions to be fought out between ignorant change on one hand, and ignorant opposition to change on the other."

The saving grace of America lies in the fact that the overwhelming majority of Americans are possessed of two great qualities—a sense of humor and a sense of proportion. With the one they smile at those who would divide up all the money in the Nation on a per capita basis every Saturday night and at those who lament that they would rather possess pounds and francs than dollars. With our sense of proportion we understand and accept the fact that in the short space of one year we cannot cure the chronic illness that beset us for a dozen years, nor restore the social and economic order with equal and simultaneous success in every part of the Nation and in every walk of life.

It is the pioneering spirit and understanding perspective of the people of the United States which already is making itself felt among other nations of the world. The simple translation of the peaceful and neighborly purposes of the United States has already given to our sister American republics a greater faith in our professions of friendship than they have held since the time, over a century ago, when James Monroe encouraged them in their struggles for freedom. So, too, I have had an example of the effect of honest statement and simple explanation of the fundamental American policy during the past week in Washington. For sixteen long years a nation, larger even than ours in population and extent of territory, has been unable to speak officially with the United States or to maintain normal relations. I believe sincerely that the most impelling motive that has lain behind the conversations which were successfully concluded yesterday between Russia and the United States was the desire of both countries for peace and for the strengthening of the peaceful purpose of the civilized world.

It will interest you to know that in the year 1809 the President of the United States, Thomas Jefferson, wrote as follows to his Russian friend, Monsieur Dashkoff:

"Russia and the United States being in character and practice essentially pacific, a common interest in the rights of peaceable nations gives us a common cause in their maintenance."

In this spirit of Thomas Jefferson, Mr. Litvinoff and I believe that through the resumption of normal relations the prospects of peace over all the world are greatly strengthened.

Furthermore, I am confident that in a State like Georgia, which had its roots in religious teachings and was the first State in which a Sunday school was established, there must be satisfaction to know that from now on any American sojourning among the great Russian people will be free to worship God in his own way.

It is perhaps especially significant that I should

speak of the resumption of relations with Russia in the city from which a century ago the first transatlantic steamship set out on its voyage to the Old World.

I am glad to be back on Georgia soil. I am hurrying to Warm Springs with special interest, for I shall see a splendid new building, given to the cause of helping crippled children by the citizens of the State of Georgia. And I am hurrying back to my cottage there for the almost equally important objective of seeing to it that a prize Georgia turkey is put into the primest possible condition for the Thanksgiving Day feast.

On this Thanksgiving, I like to think that many more fathers and mothers and children will partake of turkey than for many years past. What a splendid thing it would be if in every community throughout the land, in celebration of this Thanksgiving—and here in Georgia in celebration of the Bicentennial of the founding of the Colony—every community would set as its Thanksgiving Day objective the providing of a Thanksgiving dinner for those who have not yet been blessed by the returning prosperity sufficiently to provide their own.

Let me read to you in closing a message delivered a generation ago by a great son of a great Georgia mother, Theodore Roosevelt:

"Materially we must strive to secure a broader economic opportunity for all men so that each shall have a better chance to show the stuff of which he is made. Spiritually and ethically we must strive to bring about clean living and right thinking. We appreciate that the things of the body are important; but we appreciate also that the things of the soul are immeasurably more important. The foundation stone of national life is and ever must be the high individual character of the individual citizen."

December fifth was a historic day because of the Proclamation that the Eighteenth Amendment to the Constitution had been repealed.

On December sixth, I spoke in Washington before the Federal Council of Churches of Christ of America:

I am honored by the privilege of speaking to the delegated representatives of twenty-five Christian denominations assembled here on the twenty-fifth anniversary of the Federal Council of Churches of Christ in America. In this quarter of a century you have surrendered no individual creed, but at the same time you have been creating a much needed union that seeks to better the social and moral conditions of all the people of America.

During a quarter of a century more greatly controlled by the spirit of conquest and greed than any similar period since the American and the French revolutions you have survived and grown. You have come through to the threshold of a new era in which your churches and the other churches —Gentile and Jew—recognize and stand ready to lead in a new war of peace—the war for social justice.

Christianity was born in and of an era notable for the great gulf that separated the privileged from the under-privileged of the world of two thousand years ago—an era of lines of demarcation between conquerors and conquered; between caste and caste; between warring philosophies based on the theories of logicians rather than on practical humanities. The early churches were united in a social ideal.

Although through all the centuries we know of many periods when civilization has slipped a step backward, yet I am confident that over the sum of the centuries we have gained many steps for every one we have lost.

Now, once more, we are embarking on another voyage into the realm of human contacts. That human agency which we call government is seeking through social and economic means the same goal which the churches are seeking through social and spiritual means.

If I were asked to state the great objective which church and state are both demanding for the sake of every man and woman and child in this country, I would say that that great objective is "a more abundant life."

The early Christians challenged the pagan ethics of Greece and of Rome; we are wholly ready to challenge the pagan ethics that are represented in many phases of our boasted modern civilization. We have called on enlightened business judgment, on understanding labor and on intelligent agriculture to provide a more equitable balance of the abundant life between all elements of the community.

We recognize the right of the individual to seek and to obtain his own fair wage, his own fair profit, in his own fair way—just so long as in the doing of it he shall not push down nor hold down his own neighbor. And at the same time, we are at one in calling for collective effort on broad lines of social planning—a collective effort which is wholly in accord with the social teachings of Christianity.

This new generation of ours stands ready to help us. They may not be as ready as were their fathers and mothers to accept the outward requirements or even many of the ancient observances of the several churches, yet I truly believe that these same churches can find in them a stronger support for the fundamentals of social betterment than many of the older generation are willing to concede.

This younger generation is not satisfied with the

exposure of those in high places who seek to line their own nests with other people's money, to cheat their government of its just dues or to break the spirit of the law while observing its legalistic letter. This new generation seeks action—action by collective government and by individual education—toward the ending of practices such as these.

This new generation, for example, is not content with preachings against that vile form of collective murder—lynch law—which has broken out in our midst anew. We know that it is murder, and a deliberate and definite disobedience of the Commandment, "Thou shalt not kill." We do not excuse those in high places or in low who condone lynch law.

But a thinking America goes further. It seeks a government of its own that will be sufficiently strong to protect the prisoner and at the same time to crystallize a public opinion so clear that government of all kinds will be compelled to practice a more certain justice. The judicial function of government is the protection of the individual and of the community through quick and certain justice. That function in many places has fallen into a sad state of disrepair. It must be a part of our program to re-establish it.

From the bottom of my heart I believe that this beloved country of ours is entering upon a time of great gain. That gain can well include a greater material prosperity if we take care that it is a prosperity for a hundred and twenty million human beings and not a prosperity for the top of the pyramid alone. It can be a prosperity socially controlled for the common good. It can be a prosperity built on spiritual and social values rather than on special privilege and special power.

Toward that new definition of prosperity the churches and the governments, while wholly separate in their functioning, can work hand in hand. Government can ask the churches to stress in their teaching the ideals of social justice, while at the same time government guarantees to the churches —Gentile and Jew—the right to worship God in their own way. The churches, while they remain wholly free from even the suggestion of interference in government, can at the same time teach their millions of followers that they have the right to demand of the government of their own choosing, the maintenance and furtherance of "a more abundant life." State and church are rightly united in a common aim. With the help of God, we are on the road toward it.

Just before Christmas, action was taken by Proclamation to carry out the world silver agreement entered into at the London Economic Conference. Not only did the United States Treasury offer to purchase the quota assigned to it by the

Conference agreement, but at the same time we offered a net price of 64½ cents an ounce for all silver mined in this country, thus greatly rehabilitating a widespread industry.

I issued a Christmas Amnesty Proclamation extending a full pardon to all persons who had been convicted under the Espionage Act and the Selective Service Act during the World War and who had complied with the sentences imposed upon them.

The year 1933 drew to a close in a Christmas and New Year season which meant a larger degree of general happiness in every part of the land than we had had for many years. Deeper than the increase of prosperity, deeper than the Christmas buying, deeper even than the providing of work in almost every community, lay the fact of the spirit of the Nation. In the best sense, we had definitely started to come back.

The turn of the year brought to me the sad news that my good friend, Secretary of the Treasury Woodin, must resign his post because of continued ill health. Every member of the official family, high and low, regretted his leaving us. I was happy, however, to be able to appoint in his place my associate of many years, Henry Morgenthau Jr., who during the first part of the Administration had been the head of the Farm Credit Administration and later had been Under Secretary and Acting Secretary of the Treasury.

CHAPTER ELEVEN

THE new year opened with the advent of the Congress. It was good to welcome the Vice President, the Speaker, and many other old friends on their return to the capital. On January third, I delivered in person the following message to the Congress, assembled in Joint Session:

I come before you at the opening of the Regular Session of the Seventy-third Congress, not to make requests for special or detailed items of legislation; I come, rather, to counsel with you, who, like myself, have been selected to carry out a mandate of the whole people, in order that without partisanship you and I may co-operate to continue the restoration of our national well-being and, equally important, to build on the ruins of the past a new structure designed better to meet the present problems of modern civilization.

Such a structure includes not only the relations of industry and agriculture and finance to each other but also the effect which all of these three have on our individual citizens and on the whole people as a nation.

Now that we are definitely in the process of recovery, lines have been rightly drawn between those to whom this recovery means a return to old methods—and the number of these people is small—and those for whom recovery means a reform of many old methods, a permanent readjustment of many of our ways of thinking and therefore of many of our social and economic arrangements.

Civilization cannot go back: civilization must not stand still. We have undertaken new methods. It is our task to perfect, to improve, to alter when necessary, but in all cases to go forward. To consolidate what we are doing, to make our economic and social structure capable of dealing with modern life is the joint task of the legislative, the judicial, and the executive branches of the National Government.

Without regard to party, the overwhelming majority of our people seek a greater opportunity for humanity to prosper and find happiness. They recognize that human welfare has not increased and does not increase through mere materialism and luxury, but that it does progress through integrity, unselfishness, responsibility and justice.

In the past few months, as a result of our action, we have demanded of many citizens that they surrender certain licenses to do as they please in their business relationships; but we have asked this in exchange for the protection which the State can give against exploitation by their fellow men or by combinations of their fellow men.

I congratulate this Congress upon the courage, the earnestness and the efficiency with which you met the crisis at the Special Session. It was your fine understanding of the national problem that furnished the example which the country has so splendidly followed. I venture to say that the task confronting the First Congress of 1789 was no greater than your own.

I shall not attempt to set forth either the many phases of the crisis which we experienced last March, nor the many measures which you and I undertook during the Special Session that we might initiate recovery and reform.

It is sufficient that I should speak in broad terms of the results of our common counsel.

The credit of the Government has been fortified by drastic reduction in the cost of its permanent agencies through the Economy Act.

With the two-fold purpose of strengthening the whole financial structure and of arriving eventually at a medium of exchange which will have over the years less variable purchasing and debt-paying power for our people than that of the past, I have used the authority granted me to purchase all American produced gold and silver and to buy additional gold in the world markets. Careful investigation and constant study prove that in the matter of foreign exchange rates certain of our sister nations find themselves so handicapped by internal and other conditions that they feel unable at this time to enter into stabilization discussion based on permanent and world-wide objectives.

The overwhelming majority of the banks, both national and State, which reopened last spring, are in sound condition and have been brought within the protection of Federal Insurance. In the case of those banks which were not permitted to reopen, nearly 600 million dollars of frozen deposits are being restored to the depositors through the assistance of the National Government.

We have made great strides towards the objectives of the National Industrial Recovery Act, for not only have several millions of our unemployed been restored to work, but industry is organizing itself with a greater understanding that reasonable profits can be earned while at the same time protection can be assured to guarantee to labor adequate pay and proper conditions of work. Child labor is abolished. Uniform standards of hours and wages apply today to 95 per cent of industrial employment within the field of the National Industrial Recovery Act. We seek the definite end of preventing combinations in furtherance of monopoly and in restraint of trade, while at the same time we seek to prevent ruinous rivalries within industrial groups which in many cases resemble the gang wars of the underworld and in which the real victim in every case is the public itself.

Under the authority of this Congress, we have brought the component parts of each industry together around a common table, just as we have brought problems affecting labor to a common meeting ground. Though the machinery, hurriedly devised, may need readjustment from time to time, nevertheless I think you will agree with me that we have created a permanent feature of our modernized industrial structure and that it will continue under the supervision but not the arbitrary dictation of government itself.

You recognized last spring that the most serious part of the debt burden affected those who stood in danger of losing their farms and their homes. I am glad to tell you that refinancing in both of these cases is proceeding with good success and in all probability within the financial limits set by the Congress.

But agriculture had suffered from more than its debts. Actual experience with the operation of the Agricultural Adjustment Act leads to my belief that thus far the experiment of seeking a balance between production and consumption is succeeding and has made progress entirely in line with reasonable expectations towards the restoration of farm prices to parity. I continue in my conviction that industrial progress and prosperity can only be attained by bringing the purchasing power of that portion of our population which in one form or another is dependent upon agriculture up to a level which will restore a proper balance between every section of the country and every form of work.

In this field, through carefully planned flood control, power development and land use policies, in the Tennessee Valley and in other great watersheds, we are seeking the elimination of waste, the removal of poor lands from agriculture and the encouragement of small local industries, thus furthering this principle of a better balanced national life. We recognize the great ultimate cost of the application of this rounded policy to every part of the Union. Today we are creating heavy obligations to start the work and because of the great unemployment needs of the moment. I look forward, however, to the time in the not distant future, when annual appropriations, wholly covered by current revenue, will enable the work to proceed with a national plan. Such a national plan will, in a generation or two, return many times the money spent on it; more important, it will eliminate the use of inefficient tools, conserve and increase natural resources, prevent waste, and enable millions of our people to take better advantage of the opportunities which God has given our country.

I cannot, unfortunately, present to you a picture of complete optimism regarding world affairs.

The delegation representing the United States has worked in close co-operation with the other American republics assembled at Montevideo to make that conference an outstanding success. We have, I hope, made it clear to our neighbors that we seek with them future avoidance of territorial expansion and of interference by one nation in the internal affairs of another. Furthermore, all of us are seeking the restoration of commerce in ways which will preclude the building up of large favorable trade balances by any one nation at the expense of trade debits on the part of other nations.

In other parts of the world, however, fear of immediate or future aggression and with this the spending of vast sums on armament and the continued building up of defensive trade barriers prevent any great progress in peace or trade agreements. I have made it clear that the United States cannot take part in political arrangements in Europe but that we stand ready to co-operate at any time in practicable measures on a world basis looking to immediate reduction of armaments and the lowering of the barriers against commerce.

I expect to report to you later in regard to debts owed the Government and people of this country by the governments and peoples of other countries. Several nations, acknowledging the debt, have paid in small part; other nations have failed to pay. One nation—Finland—has paid the installments due this country in full.

Returning to home problems, we have been shocked by many notorious examples of injuries done our citizens by persons or groups who have been living off their neighbors by the use of methods either unethical or criminal.

In the first category—a field which does not involve violations of the letter of our laws—practices have been brought to light which have shocked those who believed that we were in the past generation raising the ethical standards of business. They call for stringent preventive or regulatory measures. I am speaking of those individuals who have evaded the spirit and purpose of our tax laws, of those high officials of banks or corporations who have grown rich at the expense of their stockholders or the public, of those reckless speculators with their own or other people's money whose operations have injured the values of the farmers' crops and the savings of the poor.

In the other category, crimes of organized banditry, cold-blooded shooting, lynching and kidnaping have threatened our security.

These violations of ethics and these violations of law call on the strong arm of government for their immediate suppression; they call also on the country for an aroused public opinion.

The adoption of the Twenty-first Amendment should give material aid to the elimination of those new forms of crime which came from the illegal traffic in liquor.

I shall continue to regard it as my duty to use whatever means may be necessary to supplement State, local and private agencies for the relief of suffering caused by unemployment. With respect to this question, I have recognized the dangers inherent in the direct giving of relief and have sought the means to provide not mere relief, but the opportunity for useful and remunerative work. We shall, in the process of recovery, seek to move as rapidly as possible from direct relief to publicly supported work and from that to the rapid restoration of private employment.

It is to the eternal credit of the American people that this tremendous readjustment of our national life is being accomplished peacefully, without serious dislocation, with only a minimum of injustice and with a great, willing spirit of co-operation throughout the country.

Disorder is not an American habit. Self-help and self-control are the essence of the American tradition—not of necessity the form of that tradition, but its spirit. The program itself comes from the American people.

It is an integrated program, national in scope. Viewed in the large, it is designed to save from destruction and to keep for the future the genuinely important values created by modern society. The vicious and wasteful parts of that society we could not save if we wished; they have chosen the way of self-destruction. We would save useful mechanical invention, machine production, industrial efficiency, modern means of communication, broad education. We would save and encourage the slowly growing impulse among consumers to enter the industrial market place equipped with sufficient organization to insist upon fair prices and honest sales.

But the unnecessary expansion of industrial plants, the waste of natural resources, the exploitation of the consumers of natural monopolies, the accumulation of stagnant surpluses, child labor, and the ruthless exploitation of all labor, the encouragement of speculation with other people's money, these were consumed in the fires that they themselves kindled: we must make sure that as we reconstruct our life there be no soil in which such weeds can grow again.

We have ploughed the furrow and planted the good seed; the hard beginning is over. If we would reap the full harvest, we must cultivate the soil where this good seed is sprouting and the plant is reaching up to mature growth.

A final personal word. I know that each of you will appreciate that I am speaking no mere politeness when I assure you how much I value the fine relationship that we have shared during these months of hard and incessant work. Out of these friendly contacts we are, fortunately, building a strong and permanent tie between the legislative and executive branches of the Government. The letter of the Constitution wisely declared a separation, but the impulse of common purpose declares a union. In this spirit we join once more in serving the American people.

The next day, I transmitted the Annual Budget Message to the Congress. It is, of course, filled with figures and accompanied by a huge volume containing in detail all of the proposed appropriations for running the Government during the fiscal year beginning July 1, 1934, and ending June 30, 1935. Although the facts of previous appropriations had all been made public, the country, and I think most of the Congress, did not fully realize the huge sum which would be expended by the Government this year and next year; nor did they realize the great amount the Treasury would have to borrow. Nevertheless, the budget was made so clear that we were able to look forward to the time, two years from now, when we could hope the Government would be definitely on a balanced financial basis and could look forward also to the commencement of reduction of the national debt.

On January tenth, I asked the Senate for ratification of the St. Lawrence Treaty with Canada in the following message:

I request the consideration of ratification by the Senate of the so-called St. Lawrence Treaty with Canada. Broad national reasons lead me, without hesitation, to advocate the Treaty. There are two main considerations, navigation and power.

Canada and the United States are possessed of

a natural flow of water from near the center of the continent to the ocean—a flow which throughout the greater part of its length is today available for navigation by large size vessels. A system of locks at the eastern end of Lake Superior, a dredged channel between Lake Huron and Lake Erie, and another series of great locks between Lake Erie and Lake Ontario provide free and adequate navigation to a point well down the St. Lawrence River. From there, a series of three rapids, all of them within a distance of 120 miles, now impede navigation by ocean-going vessels; but a Canadian canal already provides facilities for smaller ships. This Canadian canal now is used substantially up to its capacity.

Two of the three rapids are wholly in Canadian territory; the other is in the so-called international section. A great power development at the Beauharnois Rapids in Canada is already nearing completion and locks for ocean-going ships have been planned for and could readily be built at a low cost as part of the plan. This means that only two additional series of locks are required for a complete and continuous seaway from Duluth to salt water. I call your attention to the simple fact that Canada alone can, if desired, build locks at the Lachine Rapids and at the international sector and thus provide a seaway wholly within Canadian control without treaty participation by the United States. This, however, would be a reversal of the policy of co-operation which the

United States and Canada have continuously maintained for generations.

I want to make it very clear that this great international highway for shipping is without any question going to be completed in the near future and that this completion should be carried out by both Nations instead of by one.

I am sending you herewith a summary of data prepared at my request by governmental agencies. This summary, in its relation to the economic aspects of the seaway, shows from the broad national point of view, first, that commerce and transportation will be greatly benefited and, second, local fears of economic harm to special localities or to special interests are grossly exaggerated. It is, I believe, a historic fact that every great improvement directed to better commercial communications, whether in the case of railroads into new territory, or the deepening of great rivers, or the building of canals, or even the cutting of the Isthmus of Panama, have all been subjected to opposition on the part of local interests which conjure up imaginary fears and fail to realize that improved transportation results in increased commerce benefiting directly or indirectly all sections.

For example, I am convinced that the building of the St. Lawrence Seaway will not injure the railroads or throw their employees out of work; that it will not in any way interfere with the proper use of the Mississippi River or the Missouri River for navigation. Let us be wholly frank in saying that it is better economics to send grain or other raw materials from our Northwest to Europe via the Great Lakes and St. Lawrence than it is to send them around three sides of a square—via Texas ports or the Mississippi, thence, through the Gulf of Mexico and thence, from the southern end of the North Atlantic to its northern end. In this illustration, it is well to remember that a straight line is the shortest distance between two points.

I am satisfied that the treaty contains adequate provision for the needs of the Chicago Drainage District and for navigation between Lake Michigan and the Mississippi River. A special report from the Chief of Engineers of the War Department covers this subject.

On the affirmative side, I subscribe to the definite belief that the completion of the seaway will greatly serve the economic and transportation needs of a vast area of the United States and should, therefore, be considered solely from the national point of view.

The other great objective provided for in the treaty relates to the development of electric power. As you know, I have advocated the development of four great power areas in the United States, each to serve as a yardstick and each to be controlled by government or governmental agencies. The Tennessee Valley plants and projects in the Southeast, the Boulder Dam on the Colorado

River in the Southwest, and Columbia River projects in the Northwest are already under construction. The St. Lawrence development in the Northeast calls for action. This river is a source of incomparably cheap power located in proximity to a great industrial and rural market and within transmission distance of millions of domestic consumers.

The Legislature of the State of New York by unanimous vote set up the necessary State machinery during my term as Governor of New York and the State stands ready to co-operate with the Federal Government in the distribution of power in accordance with what I believe is today a definite national policy.

Power in the international sector of the St. Lawrence cannot be developed without a treaty between the United States and Canada. On the other hand, Canada can develop a huge block of new power at the two other rapids which lie wholly within Canadian territory. Here again, as in the case of navigation, it is better in every way that we should maintain the historic principle of accord with Canada in the mutual development of the two nations.

I have not stressed the fact that the starting of this great work will put thousands of unemployed to work. I have preferred to stress the great future advantages to our country and especially the fact that all of us should view this treaty in the light of the benefits which it confers on the people of the United States as a whole.

On January fifteenth came an exceedingly important message to the Congress asking for the establishment of a permanent policy; placing all monetary gold in the ownership of the Government as a bullion base for its currency, and at the same time, providing for a more definite determination of the gold value of the American dollar. This message, although long, is of such importance that I set it forth here in full:

In conformity with the progress we are making in restoring a fairer price level and with our purpose of arriving eventually at a less variable purchasing power for the dollar, I ask the Congress for certain additional legislation to improve our financial and monetary system. By making clear that we are establishing permanent metallic reserves in the possession and ownership of the Federal Government, we can organize a currency system which will be both sound and adequate.

The issuance and control of the medium of exchange which we call "money" is a high prerogative of government. It has been such for many centuries. Because they were scarce, because they could readily be subdivided and transported, gold and silver have been used either for money

215

or as a basis for forms of money which in themselves had only nominal intrinsic value.

In pure theory, of course, a government could issue mere tokens to serve as money—tokens which would be accepted at their face value if it were certain that the amount of these tokens was permanently limited and confined to the total amount necessary for the daily cash needs of the community. Because this assurance could not always or sufficiently be given, governments have found that reserves or bases of gold and silver behind their paper or token currency added stability to their financial systems.

There is still much confusion of thought which prevents a world-wide agreement creating a uniform monetary policy. Many advocate gold as the sole basis of currency; others advocate silver; still others advocate both gold and silver whether as separate bases, or on a basis with a fixed ratio, or on a fused basis.

We hope that, despite present world confusion, events are leading to some future form of general agreement. The recent London agreement in regard to silver was a step, though only a step, in this direction.

At this time we can usefully take a further step, which we hope will contribute to an ultimate world-wide solution.

Certain lessons seem clear. For example, the free circulation of gold coins is unnecessary, leads to hoarding, and tends to a possible weakening of national financial structures in times of emergency. The practice of transferring gold from one individual to another or from the government to an individual within a nation is not only unnecessary, but is in every way undesirable. The transfer of gold in bulk is essential only for the payment of international trade balances.

Therefore it is a prudent step to vest in the government of a nation the title to and possession of all monetary gold within its boundaries and to keep that gold in the form of bullion rather than in coin.

Because the safe-keeping of this monetary basis rests with the Government, we have already called in the gold which was in the possession of private individuals or corporations. There remains, however, a very large weight in gold bullion and coins which is still in the possession or control of the Federal Reserve Banks.

Although under existing law there is authority, by executive act, to take title to the gold in the possession or control of the Reserve Banks, this is a step of such importance that I prefer to ask the Congress by specific enactment to vest in the United States Government title to all supplies of American-owned monetary gold, with provision for the payment therefor in gold certificates. These gold certificates will be, as now, secured at all times dollar for dollar by gold in the Treasury—

gold for each dollar of such weight and fineness as may be established from time to time.

Such legislation places the right, title and ownership to our gold reserves in the Government itself; it makes clear the Government's ownership of any added dollar value of the country's stock of gold which would result from any decrease of the gold content of the dollar which may be made in the public interest. It would also, of course, with equal justice, cast upon the Government the loss of such dollar value if the public interest in the future should require an increase in the amount of gold designated as a dollar.

The title to all gold being in the Government, the total stock will serve as a permanent and fixed metallic reserve which will change in amount only so far as necessary for the settlement of international balances or as may be required by a future agreement among the nations of the world for a redistribution of the world stock of monetary gold.

With the establishment of this permanent policy, placing all monetary gold in the ownership of the Government as a bullion base for its currency, the time has come for a more certain determination of the gold value of the American dollar. Because of world uncertainties, I do not believe it desirable in the public interest that an exact value be now fixed. The President is authorized by present legislation to fix the lower limit of permissible revaluation at 50 per cent. Careful study leads me to believe that any revaluation at more than 60 per cent of the present statutory value would not be in the public interest. I, therefore, recommend to the Congress that it fix the upper limit of permissible revaluation at 60 per cent.

That we may be further prepared to bring some greater degree of stability to foreign exchange rates in the interests of our people, there should be added to the present power of the Secretary of the Treasury to buy and sell gold at home and abroad, express power to deal in foreign exchange as such. As a part of this power, I suggest that, out of the profits of any devaluation, there should be set up a fund of two billion dollars for such purchases and sales of gold, foreign exchange and government securities as the regulation of the currency, the maintenance of the credit of the Government and the general welfare of the United States may require.

Certain amendments of existing legislation relating to the purchase and sale of gold and to other monetary matters would add to the convenience of handling current problems in this field. The Secretary of the Treasury is prepared to submit information concerning such changes to the appropriate committees of the Congress.

The foregoing recommendations relate chiefly to gold. The other principal precious metal—silver—has also been used from time immemorial as a metallic base for currencies as well as for actual currency itself. It is used as such by probably half the population of the world. It constitutes a very important part of our own monetary structure. It is such a crucial factor in much of the world's international trade that it cannot be neglected.

On December 21, 1933, I issued a Proclamation providing for the coinage of our newly mined silver and for increasing our reserves of silver bullion, thereby putting us among the first nations to carry out the silver agreement entered into by sixty-six governments at the London Conference. This agreement is distinctly a step in the right direction and we are proceeding to perform our part of it.

All of the sixty-six nations agreed to refrain from melting or debasing their silver coins, to replace paper currency of small denominations with silver coins and to refrain from legislation that would depreciate the value of silver in the world markets. Those nations producing large quantities of silver agreed to take specified amounts from their domestic production and those holding and using large quantities agreed to restrict the amount they would sell during the four years covered by the agreement.

If all these undertakings are carried out by the governments concerned, there will be a marked increase in the use and value of silver.

Governments can well, as they have in the past, employ silver as a basis for currency, and I look for a greatly increased use. I am, however, withholding any recommendation to the Congress looking to further extension of the monetary use of silver because I believe that we should gain more knowledge of the results of the London agreement and of our other monetary measures.

Permit me once more to stress two principles. Our national currency must be maintained as a sound currency which, in so far as possible, will have a fairly constant standard of purchasing power and be adequate for the purposes of daily use and the establishment of credit.

The other principle is the inherent right of government to issue currency and to be the sole custodian and owner of the base or reserve of precious metals underlying that currency. With this goes the prerogative of government to determine from time to time the extent and nature of the metallic reserve. I am confident that the Nation will well realize the definite purpose of the Government to maintain the credit of that Government and, at the same time, to provide a sound medium of exchange which will serve the needs of our people.

On January nineteenth by Executive Order I further amended the regulations relating to veterans in a number of particulars and at an additional cost of twenty-one million dollars. This order affected two hundred and twenty-eight thousand veterans.

Shortly before the new year, I had set up the Federal Alcohol Control Administration with Mr. Joseph H. Choate Jr., as its director. This action provided for the interim period between the repeal of the Eighteenth Amendment and the enactment of permanent new legislation.

On January thirtieth, in over five thousand communities throughout the country, I was greatly honored by birthday parties, and at these celebrations funds were raised for the continuation and expansion of the treatment of infantile paralysis and kindred troubles at Warm Springs, Georgia. I was, of course, deeply touched by the holding of these parties, all of which were spontaneously arranged for, and by the opportunity which they afforded to make the whole Nation more conscious of the problem of its crippled children. In speaking over the radio to these gatherings that evening, I said:

Tonight I am very deeply moved by the choice of my birthday anniversary for the holding of Birthday Balls in so many communities, great and small, throughout the country. I send you my greetings and my heartfelt thanks; but at the same time I feel that I have the right to speak to you even more as a representative on this occasion of the hundreds of thousands of crippled children in our country.

It is only in recent years that we have come to realize the true significance of the problem of our crippled children. There are so many more of them than we had any idea of; in many sections there are thousands who are not only receiving no help but whose very existence has been unknown to the doctors and health services.

A generation ago somewhat the same situation existed in relation to tuberculosis. Today, because of constant stressing of the subject, the Nation understands the tuberculosis problem and has taken splendid steps not only to effectuate cures but also to prevent the spread of the disease.

The problem of the crippled child is very similar. Modern medical science has advanced so far that a very large proportion of children who for one reason or another have become crippled can be restored to useful citizenship. It remains, therefore, only to spread the gospel for the care and cure of crippled children in every part of this kindly land to enable us to make the same relative progress that we have already made in the field of tuberculosis.

As all of you know, the work at Warm Springs has been close to my heart, because of the many hundreds of cases of infantile paralysis which have been treated there. It is a fact that infantile paralysis results in the crippling of children and of grown-ups more than any other cause. Warm Springs is only one of the many places where kindness and patience and skill are given to handicapped people. There are hundreds of other places, hospitals and clinics, where the surgeons, doctors and nurses of the country gladly work day in and day out throughout the years, often without compensation.

Warm Springs, through the generous gifts which are being made to the Foundation tonight, will be able to increase its usefulness nationally, especially in the field of infantile paralysis. We shall be able to take more people and I hope that these people will be able to come to us on the recommendation of doctors from every State in the Union. I want to stress, however, that the problem of the crippled child is so great that in every community and in every State the local facilities for caring for the crippled need the support and the interest of every citizen. Let us well remember that every child and indeed every person who is restored to useful citizenship is an asset to the country and is enabled "to pull his own weight in the boat." In the long run, by helping this work we are not contributing to charity but we are contributing to the building up of a sound Nation.

At Warm Springs the facilities are available, in so far as beds and funds permit, to the rich and to the poor.

The fund to which you contribute tonight will undoubtedly permit us to extend the facilities of Warm Springs in a greater degree than before. I like to think and I would like each one of you who hears me to remember that what you are doing means the enriching of the life of some crippled child. I know and you know that there could be no finer purpose than our will to aid these helpless little ones.

Today so many thousands of welcome telegrams and postcards and letters of birthday greetings have poured in on me in the White House that I want to take this opportunity of thanking all of you who have sent them. From the bottom of my heart I am grateful to you for your thought. I wish I could divide myself by six thousand and attend in person each and every one of these birthday parties. I cannot do that, but I can be and I am with you all in spirit and in the promotion of this great cause for which we all are crusading.

No man has ever had a finer birthday remembrance from his friends and fellows than you have given me tonight. It is with an humble and thankfull heart that I accept this tribute through me to the stricken ones of our great national family. I thank you but lack the words to tell you how deeply I appreciate what you have done and I bid you good night on what is to me the happiest birthday I have ever known.

On the same day, I signed the new law relating to gold, and a Proclamation was issued the following day putting the new system into effect.

On February eighth, the following message was sent to the Congress in relation to the sugar problem. It speaks for itself:

Steadily increasing sugar production in the continental United States and in insular regions has created a price and marketing situation prejudicial to virtually everyone interested. Farmers in many areas are threatened with low prices for their beets and cane, and Cuban purchases of our goods have dwindled steadily as her shipments of sugar to this country have declined.

There is a school of thought which believes that sugar ought to be on the free list. This belief is based on the high cost of sugar to the American consuming public.

The annual gross value of the sugar crop to American beet and cane growers is approximately $60,000,000. Those who believe in the free importation of sugar say that the two cents a pound tariff is levied mostly to protect this sixty-million-dollar crop and that it costs our consuming public every year more than 200 million dollars to afford this protection.

I do not at this time recommend placing sugar on the free list. I feel that we ought first to try out a system of quotas with the three-fold object of keeping down the price of sugar to consumers, of providing for the retention of beet and cane farming within our continental limits, and also to provide against further expansion of this necessarily expensive industry.

Consumers have not benefited from the disorganized state of sugar production here and in the insular regions. Both the import tariff and cost of distribution, which together account for the major portion of the consumers' price for sugar, have remained relatively constant during the past three years.

This situation clearly calls for remedial action. I believe that we can increase the returns to our farmers, contribute to the economic rehabilitation of Cuba, provide adequate quotas for the Philippines, Hawaii, Puerto Rico and the Virgin Islands, and at the same time prevent higher prices to our own consumers.

The problem is difficult but can be solved if it is met squarely and if small temporary gains are sacrificed to ultimate general advantage.

The objective may be attained most readily through amendment of existing legislation. The

Agricultural Adjustment Act should be amended to make sugar beets and sugar cane basic agricultural commodities. It then will be possible to collect a processing tax on sugar, the proceeds of which will be used to compensate farmers for holding their production to the quota level. A tax of less than one-half cent per pound would provide sufficient funds.

Consumers need not and should not bear this tax. It is already within the executive power to reduce the sugar tariff by an amount equal to the tax. In order to make certain that American consumers shall not bear an increased price due to this tax, Congress should provide that the rate of the processing tax shall in no event exceed the amount by which the tariff on sugar is reduced below the present rate of import duty.

By further amendment to the Agricultural Adjustment Act, the Secretary of Agriculture should be given authority to license refiners, importers and handlers to buy and sell sugar from the various producing areas only in the proportion which recent marketings of such areas bear to total United States consumption. The average marketings of the past three years provide on the whole an equitable base, but the base period should be flexible enough to allow slight adjustments as between certain producing areas.

The use of such a base would allow approximately the following preliminary and temporary quotas:

	Short Tons
Continental beets	1,450,000
Louisiana and Florida	260,000
Hawaii	935,000
Puerto Rico	821,000
Philippine Islands	1,037,000
Cuba	1,944,000
Virgin Islands	5,000
	6,452,000

The application of such quotas would immediately adjust market supplies to consumption, and would provide a basis for reduction of production to the needs of the United States market.

Furthermore, in negotiations for a new treaty between the United States and Cuba to replace the existing Commercial Convention, which negotiations are to be resumed immediately, favorable consideration will be given to an increase in the existing preferential on Cuban sugars, to an extent compatible with the joint interests of the two countries.

In addition to action made possible by such legislative treaty changes, the Secretary of Agriculture already has authority to enter into codes and marketing agreements with manufacturers which would permit savings in manufacturing and distributing costs. If any agreements or codes are entered into, they should be in such form as to assure that producers and consumers share in the resulting savings.

On February ninth, I addressed the Congress in relation to the regulation of stock exchanges and commodity exchanges. This was in accordance with the mandate of the Democratic Platform of 1932.

In my message to you last March proposing legislation for Federal supervision of national traffic in investment securities I said:

"This is but one step in our broad purpose of protecting investors and depositors. It should be followed by legislation relating to the better supervision of the purchase and sale of all property dealt with on exchanges."

This Congress has performed a useful service in regulating the investment business on the part of financial houses and in protecting the investing public in its acquisition of securities.

There remains the fact, however, that outside the field of legitimate investment, naked speculation has been made far too alluring and far too easy for those who could and for those who could not afford to gamble.

Such speculation has run the scale from the individual who has risked his pay envelope or his meager savings on a margin transaction involving

stocks with whose true value he was wholly un-
familiar, to the pool of individuals or corporations with large resources, often not their own,
which sought by manipulation to raise or depress
market quotations far out of line with reason, all
of this resulting in loss to the average investor,
who is of necessity personally misinformed.

The exchanges in many parts of the country
which deal in securities and commodities conduct,
of course, a national business because their cus-
tomers live in every part of the country. The
managers of these exchanges have, it is true, often
taken steps to correct certain obvious abuses. We
must be certain that abuses are eliminated and to
this end a broad policy of national regulation is
required.

It is my belief that exchanges for dealing in
securities and commodities are necessary and of
definite value to our commercial and agricultural
life. Nevertheless, it should be our national policy
to restrict, as far as possible, the use of these exchanges for purely speculative operations.

I therefore recommend to the Congress the enactment of legislation providing for the regulation
by the Federal Government of the operations of
exchanges dealing in securities and commodities
for the protection of investors, for the safeguarding of values, and so far as it may be possible, for
the elimination of unnecessary, unwise and destructive speculation.

On February ninth, because of disclosures that the air mail contracts had been awarded under circumstances which conclusively showed irregularities amounting to collusion and illegality, the Postmaster General cancelled the contracts and the temporary duty of carrying the air mail was assigned to the War Department.

CHAPTER TWELVE

I T IS highly unsatisfactory that this book must stop instead of ending; it cannot go beyond March 4, 1934, but by the time it is printed the results of the requests for new legislation and for appropriations will in greater part be known.

Only a few other recommendations to the Congress were made before the end of the Administration's first year. On February seventeenth, an Executive Order clarified or modified the previous regulations relating to veterans' claims. On February twenty-second, the Bureau of Mines was transferred from the Department of Commerce to the Department of the Interior, subject, as in the case of similar orders, to disapproval by the Congress.

A message to the Congress on February twenty-sixth carried out another suggestion which I had made a year before. While always desirous of reducing the number of commissions not subject to direct responsibility under the Executive, I believed that for quasi-judicial purposes there could properly be three independent commissions covering the three logically distinct fields of transportation, power and communications. This message explains the general purpose and asks for the creation of a Communications Commission.

I have long felt that for the sake of clarity and effectiveness the relationship of the Federal Government to certain services known as utilities should be divided into three fields—transportation, power and communications. The problems of transportation are vested in the Interstate Commerce Commission, and the problems of power, its development, transmission and distribution, in the Federal Power Commission.

In the field of communications, however, there is today no single government agency charged with broad authority.

The Congress has vested certain authority over certain forms of communications in the Interstate Commerce Commission and there is in addition the agency known as the Federal Radio Commission.

I recommend that the Congress create a new agency to be known as the Federal Communications Commission, such agency to be vested with the authority now lying in the Federal Radio Commission and with such authority over communications as now lies with the Interstate Commerce Commission—the services affected to be all of those which rely on wires, cables or radio as a medium of transmission.

It is my thought that a new commission, such as I suggest, might well be organized this year by transferring the present authority for the control of communications of the Radio Commission and the Interstate Commerce Commission. The new body should, in addition, be given full power to investigate and study the business of existing companies and make recommendations to the Congress for additional legislation at the next session.

Three days later, I asked the Congress to take substantially the same action in relation to Home Owners Loan Corporation bonds as I had previously requested for farm mortgage bonds. In both cases the previous Session had given a government guarantee only to the interest on these bonds. We all felt that this was an anomalous situation, that the Government was, in effect, morally bound to see to it that the principal of the bonds should also be paid, and that a straight guarantee of both principal and interest was the honest course to take. Incidentally, also, the administration of the issuance of these bonds has led us to believe more firmly than ever in their soundness and in the probability that over a long period of years the Government will sustain no loss.

On March second I sent to the Congress a message of great importance. For a year it had been clear not only that American foreign trade had greatly diminished, but also that the inflexible provisions of a tariff law passed in 1930 prevented the increase of our trade through reciprocal agreements. Everyone who knows the history of the making and passing of general tariff legislation by the Congress realizes that especially in a world period of rapidly changing conditions, a greater flexibility than that afforded by congressional action is essential.

The legislation which I proposed did not take away from the Congress the constitutional duty of making tariff laws; the decisions of the Supreme Court give to the Executive limited and temporary authority to make certain well-defined changes within a well-defined scope. The message was as follows:

I am requesting the Congress to authorize the Executive to enter into executive commercial agreements with foreign nations; and in pursuance thereof, within carefully guarded limits, to modify existing duties and import restrictions in such a way as will benefit American agriculture and industry.

This action seems opportune and necessary at this time for several reasons.

First, world trade has declined with startling

rapidity. Measured in terms of the volume of goods in 1933, it has been reduced to approximately 70 per cent of its 1929 volume; measured in terms of dollars, it has fallen to 35 per cent. The drop in the foreign trade of the United States has been even sharper. Our exports in 1933 were but 52 per cent of the 1929 volume, and 32 per cent of the 1929 value.

This has meant idle hands, still machines, ships tied to their docks, despairing farm households, and hungry industrial families. It has made infinitely more difficult the planning for economic readjustment in which the Government is now engaged.

You and I know that the world does not stand still; that trade movements and relations once interrupted can with the utmost difficulty be restored; that even in tranquil and prosperous times there is a constant shifting of trade channels.

How much greater, how much more violent is the shifting in these times of change and of stress is clear from the record of current history. Every nation must at all times be in a position quickly to adjust its taxes and tariffs to meet sudden changes and avoid severe fluctuations in both its exports and its imports.

You and I know, too, that it is important that the country possess within its borders a necessary diversity and balance to maintain a rounded national life, that it must sustain activities vital to national defense and that such interests cannot be sacrificed for passing advantage. Equally clear is the fact that a full and permanent domestic recovery depends in part upon a revived and strengthened international trade and that American exports cannot be permanently increased without a corresponding increase in imports.

Second, other governments are to an ever-increasing extent winning their share of international trade by negotiated reciprocal trade agreements. If American agricultural and industrial interests are to retain their deserved place in this trade, the American Government must be in a position to bargain for that place with other governments by rapid and decisive negotiation based upon a carefully considered program, and to grant with discernment corresponding opportunities in the American market for foreign products supplementary to our own.

If the American Government is not in a position to make fair offers for fair opportunities, its trade will be superseded. If it is not in a position at a given moment rapidly to alter the terms on which it is willing to deal with other countries, it cannot adequately protect its trade against discriminations and against bargains injurious to its interests. Furthermore a promise to which prompt effect cannot be given is not an inducement which can pass current at par in commercial negotiations.

For this reason, any smaller degree of authority in the hands of the Executive would be ineffective.

The executive branches of virtually all other important trading countries already possess some such power.

I would emphasize that quick results are not to be expected. The successful building up of trade without injury to American producers depends upon a cautious and gradual evolution of plans.

The disposition of other countries to grant an improved place to American products should be carefully sounded and considered; upon the attitude of each must somewhat depend our future course of action. With countries which are unwilling to abandon purely restrictive national programs, or to make concessions towards the re-establishment of international trade, no headway will be possible.

The exercise of the authority which I propose must be carefully weighed in the light of the latest information so as to give assurance that no sound and important American interest will be injuriously disturbed. The adjustment of our foreign trade relations must rest on the premise of undertaking to benefit and not to injure such interests. In a time of difficulty and unemployment such as this, the highest consideration of the position of the different branches of American production is required.

From the policy of reciprocal negotiation which is in prospect, I hope in time that definite gains will result to American agriculture and industry.

Important branches of our agriculture, such as cotton, tobacco, hog products, rice, cereal and fruit-raising, and those branches of American industry whose mass production methods have led the world, will find expanded opportunities and productive capacity in foreign markets, and will thereby be spared in part, at least, the heartbreaking readjustments that must be necessary if the shrinkage of American foreign commerce remains permanent.

A resumption of international trade cannot but improve the general situation of other countries, and thus increase their purchasing power. Let us well remember that this in turn spells increased opportunity for American sales.

Legislation such as this is an essential step in the program of national economic recovery which the Congress has elaborated during the past year. It is part of an emergency program necessitated by the economic crisis through which we are passing. It should provide that the trade agreements shall be terminable within a period not to exceed three years; a shorter period probably would not suffice for putting the program into effect. In its execution, the Executive must, of course, pay due heed to the requirements of other branches of our recovery program, such as the National Industrial Recovery Act.

I hope for early action. The many immediate

situations in the field of international trade that today await our attention can thus be met effectively and with the least possible delay.

The final message of the first year in office related to granting independence to the people of the Philippine Islands. This message, after many conferences held with leaders of the Filipino people, sought to afford to them the opportunity at their coming general election to pass on the whole subject by popular vote. It proposed to re-enact the provisions for the transitory period leading up to complete independence and it repeated the trade provisions of the Act of 1933. I proposed only two changes: the first was the definite abandonment of the right of the United States to maintain army bases in the Philippines after independence; and the second suggested that the matter of permanent naval bases be left to future conferences. I said to the Congress:

Over a third of a century ago the United States, as a result of a war which had its origin in the Caribbean Sea, acquired sovereignty over the Philippine Islands, which lie many thousands of miles from our shores across the widest of oceans. Our Nation covets no territory; it desires to hold no people over whom it has gained sovereignty through war against their will.

In keeping with the principles of justice and in keeping with our traditions and aims, our Government for many years has been committed by law to ultimate independence for the people of the Philippine Islands whenever they should establish a suitable government capable of maintaining that independence among the nations of the world. We have believed that the time for such independence is at hand.

A law passed by the Seventy-second Congress over a year ago was the initial step, providing the methods, conditions and circumstances under which our promise was to be fulfilled. That Act provided that the United States would retain the option of keeping certain military and naval bases in the Islands after actual independence had been accomplished.

As to the military bases, I recommend that this provision be eliminated from the law and that these bases be relinquished simultaneously with the accomplishment of final Philippine independence.

As to the naval bases, I recommend that the law be so amended as to provide for the ultimate settlement of this matter on terms satisfactory to our own Government and that of the Philippine Islands.

I do not believe that other provisions of the original law need be changed at this time. Where imperfections or inequalities exist, I am confident that they can be corrected after proper hearing and in fairness to both peoples.

May I emphasize that while we desire to grant complete independence at the earliest proper moment, to effect this result without allowing sufficient time for necessary political and economic adjustments would be a definite injustice to the people of the Philippine Islands themselves little short of a denial of independence itself. To change, at this time, the economic provisions of the previous law would reflect discredit on ourselves.

In view of the fact that the time element is involved, I suggest that the law be amended as I have above suggested and that the time limit for the acceptance of the law by the proper authorities and by the people of the Philippine Islands be sufficiently extended to permit them to reconsider it.

For thirty-six years the relations between the people of the Philippine Islands and the people of the United States have been friendly and of great mutual benefit. I am confident that if this legislation is passed by the Congress and accepted by the Philippines we shall increase the mutual regard between the two peoples during the transition period. After the attainment of actual independence by them, friendship and trust will live.

March third marked the closing day of our first year in Washington. I attended the installation of Dr. Joseph Gray as Chancellor of American University and received an honorary degree. The address follows:

It is very delightful to me to become today an alumnus of American University. I am honored also in the association with your new Chancellor which it affords.

It is a good thing for our American life that this University should be situated in the capital of the country. It is good in the opportunity which it gives to higher education to come into a more intimate understanding of the problems of what we call government; it is good for government to expand its associations with the teachers and pupils of a liberal institution.

It is, of course, natural that I should take special interest in the announcement of the creation of a School of Public Affairs by American University. Many articles have been written, many speeches are being made which seek to review and to estimate the history of the United States during the past year. I am willing to hazard the guess that few of these epitomes will stress what to me stands out as one of the most salient features of a salient year in our American life.

I speak of the amazing and universal increase in the intelligent interest which the people of the United States are taking in the whole subject of government. In cities, in hamlets and on farms men and women in their daily contacts are discussing, as never before except in time of war, the methods by which community and national problems are ordered; and war is not, in the true sense, an exception because in such case there is but a single objective.

In the broader problem of government of all kinds, local and State and Federal and international, we in this country today are thinking not merely in terms of the moment, but in terms that apply to the rest of our lives and to the lives of our children. It is true that the immediate cause of this logical and deep-seated interest was a crisis—an immediate crisis which broke over our heads a year ago. It would have been possible perhaps for all of us to have sought only a temporary cure for the immediate illness of the Nation. We can be thankful that we have studied and are engaged in the process of eradicating the deeper causes of that illness and of many other illnesses of the body politic.

In so doing, we need very definitely practical contacts between the collegiate and educational world and the operations of government. The development of our economic life requires the intelligent understanding of the hundreds of complicated elements in our society. Government needs very definitely not only the sociological and economic points of view, but also the practical assistance of men and women who represent the academic, the business, and the professional elements in the community.

We need a trained personnel in government. We need disinterested, as well as broad-gauged public officials. This part of our problem we have not yet solved, but it can be solved and it can be accomplished without the creation of a national bureaucracy which would dominate the national life of our governmental system.

That is why I am especially happy in the announcement of the establishment of this School of Public Affairs. I can assure you of the hearty co-operation of the Administration. In the conduct of this school the more widely you can draw on every part of the Nation for the membership of its student body, the greater will be its influence in the dissemination of knowledge of government throughout the country.

Among our universities, you are young: you have a great future—a great opportunity for initiative, for constructive thinking, for practical idealism and for national service.

In this address I touched for the first time on a subject which necessarily attends a government policy of an expanding partnership with agriculture, industry, and finance. Ever since I knew Grover Cleveland when I was a boy, I have been a deep believer in the principles of civil service.

Nevertheless, as constituted in our country, the civil service has had very definite ups and downs. Its efficiency has not always been of the highest, nor has it been sufficiently elastic to expand in times of emergency. Building on it as a foundation, I believe that it will be possible for this country to work out a system of public service that will be at least as honest and efficient as the British Civil Service, and that will have more initiative and adaptability. Our public service must never become the kind of permanent bureaucracy which so greatly dominates the processes of government in several other countries. It must be protected in its tenure but it must not lose its initiative.

Here is an example of an opportunity that we still have before us—an opportunity to improve government service, to lessen partisanship in that service and to give, especially to the younger men and women, the chance to take part in practical government work.

CHAPTER THIRTEEN

I COULD not close this book without expressing a little more clearly than I have ever attempted to do before my thoughts concerning the responsibility of people who are in positions of authority over others.

Authority is not confined to government. It applies to the whole field of industry, labor and finance. There are many more people in positions of authority in private life than in government service. All organized life, private and public, depends upon the authority of some over others and the fineness and durability of that life depend upon the integrity with which authority is exercised.

Let us consider first those in places of public authority. President Cleveland will be best remembered through the ages for the rugged honesty of his challenging principle that "public office is a public trust." His staunch devotion to the elimination of the older doctrine that "to the victor belong the spoils" laid the foundation for a new ideal of public service in the Federal Government. As a result of the growth of this ideal the overwhelming majority of Federal public servants are honest, and this includes the men and women who are in positions of authority over these servants. I am enough of an optimist to believe that this ideal of public honesty established in the Federal service is extending slowly but surely to local government. Each year that passes sees the elimination of more and more local political machines and bosses whose chief function in life has been to feather their own nests.

Under a perfect party system of government a bid for public favor should rest solely upon political principles and good administration. We should seek through every possible means to move toward that objective. In these days the voters—especially the younger voters—are bringing us closer and closer to that ideal. They are less and less concerned with mere party emblems. They are saying more and more, "I belong to this or that party, but actually I almost always split my ticket." That is a happy sign for the future of America.

Many cynics will continue to suggest that politics is a dirty business whatever way you look at it. These cynics contribute greatly to the evils at which they sneer.

We do not want cynics in politics: we do want an ever increasing number of men and women who will take active and practical part in public affairs, in order that the level of honesty that has risen a great deal during the past fifty years may rise still further.

It is time now to add a companion to Cleveland's ideal of public service.

That companion is: Private office is a public trust.

Why, in all common sense, should we apply one rule to government and another rule to private business and the private professions? After all, there is very little distinction, so far as the effect on human beings is concerned, between the use of the authority of an alderman or a supervisor who rules over a thousand citizens, and that of the president of a company who rules over a thousand employees and stockholders. In neither case am I thinking of graft: I refer to something more important—conduct based on good ethics and good morals.

I do not indict all business executives, all labor leaders, all editors, all lawyers. But I do indict the ethics of many of them and I indict those citizens whose easy consciences condone such wrongdoing.

A new public conscience joins in this indictment. It condemns business executives who put profits ahead of human lives, who do not hesitate by unfair practices to throw a rival and his employees out of work, who speculate on inside information, who profit by deceiving the public with wrong information or who sell watered stock to innocent purchasers.

It condemns labor leaders who seek petty graft or who strive for absolute power over the actions of workers who have the right to be free and independent. It has come to suspect and to lose faith in editors who color their news stories, who put personal or party advantage ahead of a broader patriotism.

It condemns lawyers who accept retainers to find loopholes in the letter of the law as well as those who employ such lawyers. Public sentiment which once found amusement in the cleverness of those who "got away with it," is becoming less and less patient with wrongdoing, whether it is based on deliberate and serious criminality or mere cleverness. It condemns such practices whether it "succeeds" or not, and, equally important, whether it is in private business or public affairs.

Vision is an essential in all service—some quality of the mind which is never satisfied with things as they are—some quality that achieves an immediate objective and proceeds forthwith to gain the next. It is only the cynic whom I have just described as a poor citizen who will suggest that the man or woman of vision is "impractical." The idealist is not of necessity a wretched executive. Some of the greatest administrators are people who are constantly seeking better things for mankind.

In the official family of my administration the nation has been fortunate in being served by men and women of ideals and practical vision. I personally am happy in the loyal service of the members of my Cabinet from Secretary Hull through the entire list, in the devotion of the heads of the great new agencies of the Government which are helping to lift America out of the depths, in the many men and women in all branches of the Federal Government who are essential and appreciated members of the team. I am fortunate in the unselfish loyalty and help given me by those like Howe and McIntyre and Early and Moley, whose varied services I call upon at any hour of the day or night.

But the country is fortunate, not alone because of the devotion of the many people who are running "your Government," but chiefly because these persons have good minds, and are using their minds to achieve visions and ideals for the permanent benefit of the average citizen.

APPENDIX

For the sake of the record and because I find a number of variations in texts of the Inaugural Address which have been heretofore published, the text here given is the correct one.

INAUGURAL ADDRESS

OF

FRANKLIN D. ROOSEVELT

Delivered at the Capitol
Washington, D. C.
March 4, 1933

This is a day of national consecration. I am certain that on this day my fellow Americans expect that on my induction into the Presidency I will address them with a candor and a decision which the present situation of our people impels.

This is pre-eminently the time to speak the truth, the whole truth, frankly and boldly. Nor need we shrink from honestly facing conditions in our country today. This great Nation will endure as it has endured, will revive and will prosper. So, first of all, let me assert my firm belief that the only thing we have to fear is fear itself—nameless, unreasoning, unjustified terror which paralyzes needed efforts to convert retreat into advance.

In every dark hour of our national life a leadership of frankness and of vigor has met with that understanding and support of the people themselves which is essential to victory. I am convinced that you will again give that support to leadership in these critical days.

In such a spirit on my part and on yours we face our common difficulties. They concern, thank God, only material things. Values have shrunk to fantastic levels; taxes have risen; our ability to pay has fallen; government of all kinds is faced by serious curtailment of income; the means of exchange are frozen in the currents of trade; the withered leaves of industrial enterprise lie on every side; farmers find no markets for their produce; the savings of many years in thousands of families are gone.

More important, a host of unemployed citizens faces the grim problem of existence, and an equally great number toil with little return. Only a foolish optimist can deny the dark realities of the moment.

Yet our distress comes from no failure of substance. We are stricken by no plague of locusts. Compared with the perils which our forefathers conquered because they believed and were not afraid, we have still much to be thankful for. Nature still offers her bounty, and human efforts have multiplied it. Plenty is at our doorstep, but a generous use of it languishes in the very sight of the supply.

Primarily this is because the rulers of the exchange of mankind's goods have failed, through their own stubbornness and their own incompetence, have admitted their failure, and have abdicated. Practices of the unscrupulous money changers stand indicted in the court of public opinion, rejected by the hearts and minds of men.

True they have tried, but their efforts have been cast in the pattern of an outworn tradition. Faced by failure of credit they have proposed only the lending of more money. Stripped of the lure of profit by which to induce our people to follow their false leadership, they have resorted to exhortations, pleading tearfully for restored confidence. They only know the rules of a generation of self-seekers. They have no vision, and when there is no vision the people perish.

Yes, the money changers have fled from their high seats in the temple of our civilization. We may now restore that temple to the ancient truths. The measure of the restoration lies in the extent to which we apply social values more noble than mere monetary profit.

Happiness lies not in the mere possession of money; it lies in the joy of achievement, in the thrill of creative effort. The joy and the moral stimulation of work no longer must be forgotten in the mad chase of evanescent profits. These dark days, my friends, will be worth all they cost us if they teach us that our true destiny is not to be ministered unto but to minister to ourselves and to our fellow men.

Recognition of that falsity of material wealth as the standard of success goes hand in hand with the abandonment of the false belief that public office and high political position are to be valued only by the standards of pride of place and personal profit; and there must be an end to a conduct in banking and in business which too often has given to a sacred trust the likeness of callous and selfish wrongdoing. Small wonder that confidence languishes, for it thrives only on honesty, on honor, on the sacredness of obligations, on faithful protection, on unselfish performance: without them it can not live.

Restoration calls, however, not for changes in ethics alone. This Nation asks for action, and action now.

Our greatest primary task is to put people to work.

This is no unsolvable problem if we face it wisely and courageously. It can be accomplished in part by direct recruiting by the Government itself, treating the task as we would treat the emergency of a war, but at the same time, through this employment, accomplishing greatly needed projects to stimulate and reorganize the use of our great natural resources.

Hand in hand with this we must frankly recognize the overbalance of population in our industrial centers and, by engaging on a national scale in a redistribution, endeavor to provide a better use of the land for those best fitted for the land. The task can be helped by definite efforts to raise the values of agricultural products and with this the power to purchase the output of our cities. It can be helped by preventing realistically the tragedy of the growing loss through foreclosure of our small homes and our farms. It can be helped by insistence that the Federal, the State, and the local governments act forthwith on the demand that their cost be drastically reduced. It can be helped by the unifying of relief activities which today are often scattered, uneconomical, unequal. It can be helped by national planning for, and supervision of, all forms of transportation and of communications and other utilities that have a definitely public character. There are many ways in which it can be helped, but it can never be helped merely by talking about it. We must act; we must act quickly.

Finally, in our progress toward a resumption of work we require two safeguards against a return of the evils of the old order; there must be a strict supervision of all banking and credits and investments; there must be an end to speculation with other people's money; and there must be provision for an adequate but sound currency.

These are the lines of attack. I shall presently urge upon a new Congress, in special session, detailed measures for their fulfillment, and I shall seek the immediate assistance of the several States.

Through this program of action we address ourselves to putting our own national house in order and making income balance outgo. Our international trade relations, though vastly important, are in point of time and necessity secondary to the establishment of a sound national economy. I favor as a practical policy the putting of first things first. I shall spare no effort to restore world trade by international economic readjustment, but the emergency at home can not wait on that accomplishment.

The basic thought that guides these specific means of national recovery is not narrowly nationalistic. It is the insistence, as a first consideration, upon the interdependence of the various elements in and parts of the United States of America—a recognition of the old and permanently important manifestation of the American spirit of the pioneer. It is the way to recovery. It is the immediate way. It is the strongest assurance that recovery will endure.

In the field of world policy I would dedicate this Nation to the policy of the good neighbor—the neighbor who resolutely respects himself and, because he does so, respects the rights of others—the neighbor who respects his obligations and respects the sanctity of his agreements in and with a world of neighbors.

If I read the temper of our people correctly, we now realize as we have never realized before our interdependence on each other; that we can not merely take but we must give as well; that if we are to go forward, we must move as a trained and loyal army willing to sacrifice for

259

the good of a common discipline, because without such discipline no progress is made, no leadership becomes effective. We are, I know, ready and willing to submit our lives and our property to such discipline, because it makes possible a leadership which aims at the larger good. This I propose to offer, pledging that the larger purposes will bind upon us, bind upon us all as a sacred obligation with a unity of duty hitherto evoked only in time of armed strife.

With this pledge taken, I assume unhesitatingly the leadership of this great army of our people dedicated to a disciplined attack upon our common problems.

Action in this image, action to this end is feasible under the form of government which we have inherited from our ancestors. Our Constitution is so simple, so practical that it is possible always to meet extraordinary needs by changes in emphasis and arrangement without loss of essential form. That is why our constitutional system has proved itself the most superbly enduring political mechanism the modern world has ever seen. It has met every stress of vast expansion of territory, of foreign wars, of bitter internal strife, of world relations.

It is to be hoped that the normal balance of executive and legislative authority may be wholly adequate to meet the unprecedented task before us. But it may be that an unprecedented demand and need for undelayed action may call for temporary departure from that normal balance of public procedure.

I am prepared under my constitutional duty to recommend the measures that a stricken nation in the midst of a stricken world may require. These measures, or such other measures as the Congress may build out of its experience and wisdom, I shall seek, within my constitutional authority, to bring to speedy adoption.

But, in the event that the Congress shall fail to take one of these two courses, and in the event that the national emergency is still critical, I shall not evade the clear course of duty that will then confront me. I shall ask the Congress for the one remaining instrument to meet the crisis—broad Executive power to wage a war against the emergency, as great as the power that would be given to me if we were in fact invaded by a foreign foe.

For the trust reposed in me I will return the courage and the devotion that befit the time. I can do no less.

We face the arduous days that lie before us in the warm courage of national unity; with the clear consciousness of seeking old and precious moral values; with the clean satisfaction that comes from the stern performance of duty by old and young alike. We aim at the assurance of a rounded and permanent national life.

We do not distrust the future of essential democracy. The people of the United States have not failed. In their need they have registered a mandate that they want direct, vigorous action. They have asked for discipline and direction under leadership. They have made me the present instrument of their wishes. In the spirit of the gift I take it.

In this dedication of a Nation we humbly ask the blessing of God. May He protect each and every one of us. May He guide me in the days to come.

STATEMENT BY THE PRESIDENT

It is needless to say that the news of the death of Mayor Cermak affects me very deeply and very personally. Aside from the tragic chain of events of which his death is the result, a very warm friendship and a very high respect for Mayor Cermak's ability, friendship and loyalty to his friends would have made his loss a heavy one to me under any circumstances. The brave fight he made shows clearly the wonderful courage of the man. The country at large and the great City of Chicago in particular will miss a strong and resolute character.

March 6, 1933.

EXCERPT FROM EXECUTIVE ORDER OF APRIL 5, 1933

FORBIDDING THE HOARDING OF GOLD COIN, GOLD BULLION AND GOLD CERTIFICATES

By virtue of the authority vested in me by . . . the Act of March 9, 1933, . . . I, Franklin D. Roosevelt, President of the United States of America, do declare that said national emergency still continues to exist and pursuant to said section do hereby prohibit the hoarding of gold coin, gold bullion, and gold certificates within the continental United States. . . .

For the purposes of this regulation, the term "hoarding" means the withdrawal and withholding of gold coin, gold bullion or gold certificates from the recognized and customary channels of trade. . . .

All persons are hereby required to deliver on or before May 1, 1933, to a Federal Reserve bank or a branch or agency thereof or to any member bank of the Federal Reserve System all gold coin, gold bullion and gold certificates now owned by them or coming into their ownership, . . .

Whoever willfully violates any provision of this Executive Order or of these regulations or of any rule, regulation or license issued thereunder may be fined not more than $10,000, or, if a natural person, may be imprisoned for not more than ten years, or both; and any officer, director, or agent of any corporation who knowingly participates in any such violation may be punished by a like fine, imprisonment, or both.

EXCERPT FROM EXECUTIVE ORDER OF
APRIL 20, 1933

RELATING TO FOREIGN EXCHANGE AND THE EARMARKING AND EXPORT OF GOLD COIN OR BULLION OR CURRENCY

By virtue of the authority vested in me by . . . the Act of March 9, 1933, entitled "An Act to provide relief in the existing national emergency in banking, and for other purposes," in which amendatory Act Congress declared that a serious emergency exists, I, Franklin D. Roosevelt, President of the United States of America, do declare that said national emergency still continues to exist and pursuant to said section and by virtue of all other authority vested in me, do hereby issue the following executive order:

1. Until further order, the earmarking for foreign account and the export of gold coin, gold bullion or gold certificates from the United States or any place subject to the jurisdiction thereof are hereby prohibited, . . .

2. Until further order, the Secretary of the Treasury is authorized, through any agency that he may designate, to investigate, regulate, or prohibit, under such rules and regulations as he may prescribe, by means of licenses or otherwise, any transactions in foreign exchange, transfers of credit from any banking institution within the United States or any place subject to the jurisdiction thereof to any foreign branch or office of such banking institution or to any foreign bank or banker, and the export or withdrawal of currency from the United States or any place subject to the jurisdiction of the United States, by any individual, partnership, association, or corporation within the United States or any place subject to the jurisdiction thereof; . . .

STATEMENT BY THE PRESIDENT

On the Signing of the Farm Relief Bill

I have just signed the Farm Relief Bill which includes the refinancing of farm debts.

The Act extends relief not only to farmer borrowers but to mortgage creditors as well.

Holders of farm mortgages will have the privilege of exchanging them for Federal Land Bank bonds, the interest payments upon which are to be guaranteed by the Treasury of the United States.

Farmers whose mortgages are to be exchanged for these bonds will reap the benefit of lower interest rates and more liberal terms of payment.

It is to the interest of all the people of the United States that the benefits of this Act should be extended to all who are in need of them and that none should be deprived of them through ignorance or precipitate action.

For this reason, I appeal particularly to mortgage creditors and all others who have money claims against farmers. Every effort will be made to administer the Act promptly, considerately and justly.

All preparation that could be made in advance by officers of the Federal Land Bank System has been made. However, applications can not be acted upon instantly. Time for examination, appraisal and perfection of records will be necessary.

I urge upon mortgage creditors, therefore, until full opportunity has been given to make effective the provisions of the mortgage refinancing sections of the Farm Relief Act, that they abstain from bringing foreclosure proceedings and making any effort to dispossess farmers who are in debt to them. I invite their co-operation with the officers of the land banks, the agents of the Farm Loan Commissioner and their farmer debtors to effect agreements which will make foreclosures unnecessary.

This is in line both with public duty and private interest.

May 12, 1933.

STATEMENT BY THE PRESIDENT

On the Signing of the Emergency Unemployment Relief Bill

I want to make it very clear to citizens in every community that the Bill I have just signed, authorizing an appropriation of $500,000,000 of Federal funds for unemployment relief, does not absolve States and local communities of their responsibility to see that the necessities of life are assured their citizens who are in destitute circumstances.

The Bill in effect is a challenge to Governors, Legislatures and local officials to stimulate their own efforts to provide for their own citizens in need.

For these and other good reasons citizens who are able should voluntarily contribute to the pressing needs of welfare services.

The giving of life's necessities by the Government, in ratio to contributions made by States and local communities, should lead to the giving of generous contributions to community chests and welfare organizations throughout the country.

The principle which I have on many occasions explained is that the first obligation is on the locality: if it is absolutely clear that the locality has done its utmost but that more must be done, then the State must do its utmost. Only then can the Federal Government add its contribution to those of the locality and the State.

May 12, 1933.

EXCERPT FROM EXECUTIVE ORDER OF MAY 24, 1933, ADMITTING VETERANS TO THE CCC CAMPS

The enrollment of 25,000 veterans of the World War and veterans of previous wars be undertaken as soon as possible under supervision and such regulations as may be deemed necessary and desirable by the Director of the Emergency Conservation Work.

STATEMENT BY THE PRESIDENT

On the Signing of the Securities Act, May 27, 1933

It gives me much satisfaction to sign the Rayburn-Fletcher Securities Bill, and I know I express national feeling in congratulating Congress on its passage. For this measure at last translates some elementary standards of right and wrong into law. Events have made it abundantly clear that the merchandising of securities is really traffic in the economic and social welfare of our people. Such traffic demands the utmost good faith and fair dealing on the part of those engaged in it. If the country is to flourish, capital must be invested in enterprise. But those who seek to draw upon other people's money must be wholly candid regarding the facts on which the investor's judgment is asked.

To that end this Bill requires the publicity necessary for sound investment. It is, of course, no insurance against errors of judgment. That is the function of no government. It does give assurance, however, that, within the limit of its powers, the Federal Government will insist upon knowledge of the facts on which alone judgment can be based.

The new law will also safeguard against the abuses of high pressure salesmanship in security flotations. It will require full disclosure of all the private interests on the part of those who seek to sell securities to the public.

The Act is thus intended to correct some of the evils which have been so glaringly revealed in the private exploitation of the public's money. This law and its effective administration are steps in a program to restore some old-fashioned standards of rectitude. Without such an ethical foundation, economic well-being cannot be achieved.

RADIO ADDRESS TO THE CCC, JULY 17, 1933

In speaking to you men of the Civilian Conservation Corps, I think of you as a visible token of encouragement to the whole country. You—nearly three hundred thousand strong—are evidence that the Nation is still strong enough and broad enough to look after its citizens. You are evidence that we are seeking to get away as fast as we possibly can, from the dole; from soup kitchens and from free lodging—because the Government is paying you wages and maintaining you to do actual work—work which is needed now and for the future and will bring a definite financial return to the people of the Nation. Through you, the Nation will graduate a fine group of strong young men, clean living, trained to self-discipline and above all, willing and proud to work for the joy of working.

Too much in recent years, large numbers of our population have thought of success as an opportunity to gain money with the least possible work. It is time for each and every one of us to cast away self-destroying, Nation-destroying efforts to get something for nothing and to appreciate that satisfying rewards and safe rewards come only through honest work. That must be the new spirit of the American future. You are the vanguard of that new spirit.

RADIO ADDRESS TO GOVERNORS' CONFERENCE AT SAN FRANCISCO, JULY 25, 1933

I send my greetings across many States to the Conference of Governors assembled tonight. I wish I could meet with you and renew old and pleasant associations, created during the four years during which I was one of you. I like to recall that I was a member of the Executive Committee of the Conference of Governors and that I attended all four meetings during my term of office as Governor of New York. I found then, and subsequent observation has confirmed my belief, that the Governors' Conference is a vital and necessary organization.

I take this occasion to assure you of my deep appreciation of the co-operative spirit which you have recently shown in your resolution addressed to me. We are all engaged in the business of lifting this country from economic chaos and I congratulate you on the efforts that you are making.

I feel that one of the great problems before us is to adjust the balance between mutual State and Federal undertakings—to determine the joint responsibilities of many great tasks. I think we are making progress in this direction. There are many problems that extend beyond the power of single States. I can use as illustrations two which happen to be in the foreground in Washington at this moment:

The problem of oil production, for example, must be viewed and measured from the standpoint of the national total of production and of consumption. But, in coming to grips with the problem of limitation, the States have a function to perform which is of great importance. I am happy that the oil-producing States are co-operating with each other and with the Federal Government in this matter.

Another problem is a consideration of a wider and more effective use of the land over wide areas in such natural units as the Tennessee or the Arkansas or the Missouri or the upper Mississippi valleys. Here are problems where the individual State and regional groups of States and the Federal Government may well find possibilities of fruitful co-operation.

I extend to you a very personal note of greeting. I am more than pleased with the contacts which I have had with the Governors of the forty-eight sovereign States since I have been President. I have maintained a constant and active interchange of ideas with many of you. We have communicated by mail and telephone and more particularly by personal conferences at the White House. I hope that these contacts will continue and increase in number and importance. I hope, furthermore, that during the coming winter I may have the pleasure of meeting with you here in Washington once more and I take this occasion to extend to you a cordial invitation for such a meeting during the coming winter.

Let us look forward to this gathering in the hope that it will mark further solid accomplishments by all of us in the direction of national recovery. It is a major purpose of my Administration to strengthen the bonds between State and Federal executive authorities, to the great common ends to which we are all devoted.

My warm greetings to you all, old associates and new friends.

EXECUTIVE ORDER SETTING UP A CENTRAL STATISTICAL BOARD, JULY 27, 1933

Pursuant to the authority vested in me by Titles I and II, the National Industrial Recovery Act, Public No. 67, Seventy-third Congress, I hereby establish a Central Statistical Board to formulate standards for and to effect co-ordination of the statistical services of the Federal Government incident to the purposes of that Act. The Board shall consist of one representative designated by each of the following officers from one of the statistical agencies under his direction:

The Secretary of the Interior
The Secretary of Agriculture
The Secretary of Commerce
The Secretary of Labor
The Governor of the Federal Reserve Board
The National Industrial Recovery Administrator

and one representative to be designated by the Committee on Government Statistics and Information Services created at the invitation of the Secretaries of the Interior, Agriculture, Commerce, and Labor; and such other members as the President may designate or the Board may invite from time to time for full or limited membership.

The Board shall have the power to appraise and advise upon all schedules of all government agencies engaged in the primary collection of statistics required in carrying out the purposes of the National Industrial Recovery Act, to review plans for tabulation and classification of such statistics, and to promote the co-ordination and improvement of the statistical services involved.

The power to appoint such officers, agents and employees as it may require, is hereby delegated to the Central Statistical Board, and the Federal Emergency Administration of Public Works is hereby directed to allot to the Central Statistical Board the sum of twenty thousand dollars ($20,000) to carry out its functions.

EXECUTIVE ORDER RELATING TO THE SALE AND EXPORT OF GOLD RECOVERED FROM NATURAL DEPOSITS, AUGUST 29, 1933

By virtue of the authority vested in me by Section 5 (b) of the Act of October 6, 1917, as amended by Section 2 of the Act of March 9, 1933, entitled "An Act to provide relief in the existing national emergency in banking, and for other purposes," I, Franklin D. Roosevelt, President of the United States of America, do declare that a period of national emergency exists, and by virtue of said authority and of all other authority vested in me, do hereby issue the following Executive Order:

The Secretary of the Treasury is hereby authorized to receive on consignment for sale, subject to such rules and regulations and upon such conditions as he shall prescribe, gold recovered from natural deposits in the United States or any place subject to the jurisdiction thereof. Sales may be made:

(a) To persons licensed to acquire gold for use in the arts, industries, or professions, or

(b) By export to foreign purchasers.

Such sales shall be made at a price which the Secretary shall determine to be equal to the best price obtainable in the free gold markets of the world after taking into consideration any incidental expenses such as shipping costs and insurance.

Such sales may be made through the Federal Reserve banks or such other agents as the Secretary may from time to time designate and shall be subject to such charges as the Secretary may from time to time in his judgment determine.

Every person depositing gold for sale as provided herein shall be deemed to have agreed to accept as conclusive without any right of recourse or review, the determination of the Secretary or his duly authorized agent as to the amount due such person as a result of any sale.

Consignments shall be sold as nearly as may be in the order of their receipt.

The Secretary of the Treasury, in his discretion and subject to such regulations as he may prescribe, is hereby authorized to issue licenses permitting the export of articles fabricated from gold sold pursuant to this Executive Order.

————

This Executive Order may be modified or revoked at any time.

LETTER TO REAR ADMIRAL BYRD ON HIS DEPARTURE FOR THE ANTARCTIC, SEPTEMBER 7, 1933

MY DEAR DICK:

I am delighted that you have had the faith to go ahead with this scientific expedition to the Antarctic Continent and that you have definitely set the date of departure for September 25th.

It is because you and I are such old friends, and because I have followed so closely your three previous expeditions, that I expect to keep in close touch with your new expedition.

I realize the importance of your excellent preparations for scientific discovery, and the fact that you will make a detailed survey of a large area of new continent previously unexplored. It is worth while to serve twelve branches of science.

I am especially interested in the exhaustive study of weather on the Antarctic Continent—a territory in the clutches of the ice age, and a weather maker for the greater part of the South American Continent. Your weather observations will undoubtedly be of great importance to South America and to the scientific knowledge of world weather conditions.

From a sentimental point of view I am delighted that you are using the famous old Coast Guard revenue cutter *Bear,* and I wish much that I could see you and the expedition off when you sail.

I want you to feel that on your expedition you have the full support of United States Government and that you can call on the Government in case of need or emergency.

When you re-establish the postoffice at Little America be sure to send me a letter for my stamp collection.

Good luck to you and all of your associates and crews.

Always sincerely yours,

ADDRESS AT THE DEDICATION OF THE SAMUEL GOMPERS MEMORIAL MONUMENT, WASHINGTON, D. C., OCTOBER 7, 1933

It is fitting that in the Capital of the Nation a statue should stand through the ages, to remind future generations of the services to that Nation of a patriot who served his country well. It is fitting that the Government, through its representatives, should take part in the dedication of this monument. It is fitting that I should appear here in my official capacity; but it is also fitting that I should be here in my personal capacity, as one who has always been, proud of the personal friendship which he held for many years with Samuel Gompers.

I knew him first when as a very young man I came to New York City and received his fine support in the establishment of pure milk stations for the feeding of undernourished babies. From then on, we had many mutual tasks. It is, I think, a commentary on the progress toward social justice which we have accomplished in a short space of time, when I tell you that in the year 1911—only twenty-two years ago—Samuel Gompers, Robert F. Wagner, Alfred E. Smith and I were labeled as radicals when we fought for and finally succeeded in passing a bill through the New York State Legislature, limiting the work of women in industry to fifty-four hours a week. These early struggles for social betterment —struggles which in large part were initiated by him— have met with growing success with every passing year. I like to think that Samuel Gompers is today, and at this moment, aware of the fact that through the quick and practical action of the National Recovery Act, child labor in the United States has at last come to an end.

During the years of the Wilson Administration, the friendship between us grew and strengthened. I need not speak of his great service to organized labor in their relations with private employers; but I can speak rightfully of the splendid co-operation which at all times he gave to the sympathetic adjustment of problems relating to workers for the Government itself. He understood well the fact that those who serve the Government serve the people as a whole. It was in the fulfilment of this principle that he approached the whole subject of the relationship of labor to the Government at the outbreak of the World War. As a member of the advisory committee of the Council of National Defense, he was a part of the great organization which met the crisis of war. But more than that, it was his patriotic leadership for the unanimous mobilization of the workers in every part of the Union which supplemented the mobilization of the men who went to the front.

The keen analysis of President Wilson made this reference to Mr. Gompers, in November, 1917:

"If I may be permitted to do so I want to express my admiration of his patriotic courage, his large vision and his statesmanlike sense of what has to be done. I like to lay my mind alongside of a mind that knows how to pull in harness. The horses that kick over the traces will have to be put in a corral."

In those few words President Wilson summed up the splendid national services of Samuel Gompers, and at the same time preached a sermon that applied to capital and labor alike.

That sermon is just as good today as it was in 1917. We are engaged in another war, and I believe from the bottom of my heart that organized labor is doing its share to win this war. The whole of the country has a common enemy; industry, agriculture, capital, labor are all engaged in fighting it. Just as in 1917 we are seeking to pull in harness; just as in 1917, horses that kick over the traces will have to be put in a corral.

Mr. Gompers understood and went along with that thought during the years of the war, and we have many evidences of his acceptance of the fact that the horses pulling in harness were the horses of the employees and of the employers as well. In those years a few, happily a very few, horses had to be lassoed—both kinds of horses; and today the conditions are very similar.

In the field of organized labor there are problems just as there were in the spring of 1917—questions of jurisdiction which have to be settled quickly and effectively in order to prevent the slowing-up of the general program.

There are the perfectly natural problems of selfish individuals who seek personal gain by running counter to the calm judgment of sound leadership. There are hotheads who think that results can be obtained by noise or violence; there are insidious voices seeking to instill methods or principles which are wholly foreign to the American form of democratic government.

On the part of employers there are some who shudder at anything new. There are some who think in terms of dollars and cents instead of in terms of human lives; there are some who themselves would prefer government by a privileged class instead of by majority rule.

But it is clear that the sum of the recalcitrants on both sides cuts a very small figure in the total of employers and employees alike, who are going along whole-heartedly in the war against depression.

You of the Federation of Labor and its affiliations are in the broad sense giving the same kind of fine co-operation to your Government which Samuel Gompers and his associates gave to that same Government in the old days.

Even as in the old days when I was in the Navy Department, Mr. Gompers and the Federation were at all times on a footing of friendship and co-operation with me—even so today President Green and his associates are working with my Administration toward the attainment of our national purposes. The overwhelming majority of the workers understand, as do the overwhelming majority of the employers of the country, that this is no time to seek special privilege, undue advantage, or personal gain, because of the fact of a crisis. Like the duly constituted officials of your Government, we must put and we are putting unselfish patriotism first. That would have been the order of Samuel Gompers if he were with us today.

RADIO ADDRESS FOR THE 1933 MOBILIZATION FOR HUMAN NEEDS, OCTOBER 15, 1933

I have spoken on several occasions of the vital importance to our country that private charity in all that that broad term covers, must be kept up at least to the levels, and I hope even beyond the levels, of former years. At this opening of the Four Weeks 1933 Mobilization for Human Needs, I want not only to reaffirm what I have said before, but to stress the fact that the fine teamwork in the recovery program cannot be successful if an important horse is lying back in the traces.

It is true that I have declared that the Government must not let anyone starve this winter: but at the same time this policy is predicated on the assumption that the individual American citizen will continue to do his and her part, even more unselfishly than in the past.

Let me stress that a great many people will still need the help of relief agencies this winter. It is true that because of a partial, but I believe a steadily growing, reemployment of the unemployed, many families and many individuals have been taken off the local relief rolls. But, on the other hand, the needs of those who are still on the rolls is proportionately greater than it was before, and, in addition to the work of direct relief, it is necessary for us to continue our support of the permanent hospital and welfare services that exist in every county and in most communities.

A number—I am glad to say a small number—of people have written to me to express the thought that all relief work should be taken over by the Government, and have intimated that they would not feel any duty this year to subscribe to local relief or local charity. These people have a wholly wrong slant on the fundamental basis of our American civilization. They deny the civic responsibility of the individual, and would seek to toss every problem into the lap of Government. They are "buck passers."

On the other hand, the overwhelming majority of the American people understand clearly that it is first the duty of the individual and the local community to do all that they can to maintain relief and welfare; that it is then the obligation of the State Government to supplement local efforts, and that finally, if all of this put together is not sufficient, the Federal Government stands ready to help.

This Mobilization for Human Needs will keep the long-established hospital and welfare services going. These services existed long before the depression; they will exist long after the depression is over.

I ask every citizen to give his or her support to the community chests and to other organizations that raise funds for the regular welfare services—bodies which express the instincts of charity, of humanity and of neighborliness. They are an essential to the whole American scheme of life. Their meaning is expressed in the name—The Mobilization for Human Needs.

I am glad indeed that my old friend, Newton D. Baker, once more is heading the forces of mobilization and this time we are all happy that it is a mobilization of peace.

REMARKS TO THE GOVERNORS, MAYORS AND CIVIL WORKS ADMINISTRATORS ATTENDING THE CIVIL WORKS MEETING HELD IN THE EAST ROOM OF THE WHITE HOUSE, NOVEMBER 15, 1933

My friends, I will tell you an official secret. Harry Hopkins wrote out two and a half very excellent pages of suggestions as to what I should say. They are on the desk. I subscribe to his sentiments one hundred per cent. But, I am not going to read them.

I don't want to talk to you officially, but unofficially and extemporaneously. First of all, I want to thank you for coming here.

This group, representative of the entire country, has in its hands to accomplish something that no nation has ever before done. As you know, during the past eight months we have tried honestly and practically to face a problem that no other nation in modern history has ever been confronted with. We have heard a great deal of unemployment on the other side, in England, in France and in Germany, but at no time in any one of those countries has the unemployment situation even approximated the unemployment situation in the United States last spring. You can figure it at twelve or fourteen or sixteen million, or whatever you like—on the basis of population that is a larger percentage of men, women and children out of work—in most cases suffering physically and mentally—a larger proportion than anywhere else.

During these months a great many of our unemployed have gone back to work. The number has been estimated variously at from three and a half to five million. The actual figures make very little difference because there are still a great many, still millions, out of employment and this particular effort in which you and I are engaged at the present time is to put four million people from the list of those still unemployed back to work during the winter months so that we can honestly say as a nation that this winter is not going to be like last winter or the winter before.

I like to stress not only the fact of four million, but also the fact that of those four million of people two million are today on what we might just as well call, frankly, a dole. When any man or woman goes on a dole, something happens to them mentally and the quicker they are taken off the dole the better it is for them during the rest of their lives.

We hope we can recruit two million from the ranks of people who perhaps ought to have been on the dole—perhaps people who were too proud to ask for assistance. In every community most of us know of cases—many cases—of families that have been living along, barely subsisting, yet too proud to go and ask for relief. We want to help that type of American family.

Now this work is really and truly a partnership—a partnership between the Federal Government, the State governments and the local governments—a partnership in which each one of those three divisions is expected to and is going to do its share. This $400,000,000 isn't going to cost the Federal Government any more money, because we are taking it out of the large Public Works appropriation of $3,300,000,000. It is using a portion of that fund in a very practical way.

We might as well be perfectly frank, it has been exceedingly difficult honestly to allot the entire sum of $3,300,000,000 to worth-while projects, every one of which has had to be scanned by local authorities, State authorities and finally by the Federal Government.

I believe the question was raised this morning as to the transfer of some of the projects to which allotments have already been made by Public Works, and I have been asked by the Governor of Wyoming to clear up that point. It is possible that certain allotments already made by Secretary Ickes to Public Works may be transferred to Mr. Hopkins' Civil Works Administration.

The process, I am told, will be to have that request made to the original person who did the allotting—in other words, the Secretary of the Interior—and if he approves of the transfer, it will then be made to the Civil Works Administration under Mr. Hopkins. I think that straightens out the question the Governor of Wyoming raised.

Just one word more and I am sort of talking in the family. We have heard a good many charges and allegations that have been made in regard to relief work—the same kind of charges that were made when I was Governor of New York—charges that politics was entering into the use of Public Works funds and of emergency relief funds.

I want to tell you very, very simply that your National Government is not trying to gain political advantage one way or the other out of the needs of human beings for relief. We expect the same spirit on the part of every Governor of every one of the forty-eight States and on the part of every mayor and every county commissioner and of every relief agent. I would like to have the general rule adopted—that no person connected with the administration of this $400,000,000 will in any single case in any political subdivision of the United States ask whether a person needing relief or work is a Republican, Democrat, Socialist or anything else.

I am asking you to go ahead and do your share. Most of the work will fall on your shoulders. Most of the responsibility for the practical application of the plan will fall on you rather than on us in Washington. I can assure you that Mr. Hopkins, Secretary Ickes and all of the people connected with the Federal Government are going to co-operate in putting this plan to work quickly.

Speed is an essential. I am very confident that the mere fact of giving real wages to 4,000,000 Americans who are today not getting wages is going to do more to relieve suffering and to lift the morale of the Nation than anything undertaken before.

THANKSGIVING DAY—1933

BY THE PRESIDENT OF THE UNITED STATES OF AMERICA

A PROCLAMATION

I, Franklin D. Roosevelt, President of the United States of America, do set aside and appoint Thursday, the thirtieth day of November, 1933, to be a Day of Thanksgiving for all our people.

May we on that day in our churches and in our homes give humble thanks for the blessings bestowed upon us during the year past by Almighty God.

May we recall the courage of those who settled a wilderness, the vision of those who founded the Nation, the steadfastness of those who in every succeeding generation have fought to keep pure the ideal of equality of opportunity and hold clear the goal of mutual help in time of prosperity as in time of adversity.

May we ask guidance in more surely learning the ancient truth that greed and selfishness and striving for undue riches can never bring lasting happiness or good to the individual or to his neighbors.

May we be grateful for the passing of dark days; for the new spirit of dependence one on another; for the closer unity of all parts of our wide land; for the greater friendship between employers and those who toil; for a clearer knowledge by all nations that we seek no conquests and ask only honorable engagements by all peoples to respect the lands and rights of their neighbors; for the brighter day to which we can win through by seeking the help of God in a more unselfish striving for the common bettering of mankind.

In Witness Whereof I have hereunto set my hand and caused the seal of the United States to be affixed.

Done at the City of Washington this twenty-first day of November, in the year of our Lord Nineteen Hundred and Thirty-three and of the Independence of the United States of America the One Hundred and Fifty-eighth.

[SEAL]

ADDRESS AT THE DEDICATION OF GEORGIA HALL, WARM SPRINGS, GEORGIA, NOVEMBER 24, 1933

Most people have visions of things they would like to see accomplished; fortunate are those who with their own eyes see the accomplishment becoming a fact.

Most of you who are here tonight know the story of Warm Springs during the past nine years. You know of the hopeful handful of crippled children and adults who came seeking to walk again, and of the growth of our physical facilities and of our medical care to the point where the completion of Georgia Hall gives us a clear idea of the rounded picture of the Georgia Warm Springs of the future.

In all these years our splendid progress would have been impossible had we not had the sympathy, the understanding and the help of our neighbors; and tonight I express my appreciation and thanks, first, to you my neighbors of Warm Springs and Meriwether County, for your true friendship toward me and toward all those who have come here; and secondly, to you the people of Georgia whose welcome hospitality has culminated in this splendid gift to the Foundation and made me feel prouder than ever to call this "my other home."

It is this understanding spirit on the part of those who surround us that has contributed so greatly to what we call the "spirit of Warm Springs." No perfectly appointed hospital, no medical care of the highest skill can accomplish the best results unless at the same time we build up, as Mr. Callaway has said, confidence, self-reliance and cheerfulness on the part of the patients themselves. That is why the Warm Springs Foundation has established itself as a practical success in bringing back so many crippled children and crippled grown-ups to normal activities, and at the same time to a normal confidence in themselves.

We hear much these days of two adjectives—"social" and "economic." Generally they are used to denote different things. Here at Warm Springs we have proved that in our work they go hand in hand. Let me give you an example: If a child is so incapacitated, because of infantile paralysis or accident or some other cause, that he is unable to get about, take care of himself and go to school, the chances are that in most cases some grown-up person must spend a large part of the time in taking care of the child. Every social objective requires that the child be rehabilitated to lead a normal life—to become a useful member of society. In accomplishing this we reach at the same time the economic objective, for we restore the child and at the same time we release a member of his family from the constant supervision and care of the child, and enable that person so to be an economically useful unit in the community.

Figures show that there are well over three hundred thousand crippled children in the United States and probably at least an equal number of grown-up people. It is my belief, and I think the belief of the doctors of the United States, that the great majority of these citizens of ours, more than half a million of them, can be restored to useful citizenship if we can give them the most modern, scientific, medical and educational treatment. Toward the attainment of that goal the Georgia Warm Springs Foundation seeks to play a leading part. This work at Warm Springs is not local; people come here from every State in the Union and from many foreign countries. It is true that we can take care of only a small proportion of those who need care; but at the same time the educational value of the methods and of their results is making itself widely felt in the care of the handicapped throughout the United States.

I wish much that people all over the country could be with us here tonight to learn of the splendid effectiveness of the work we are doing; to see this beautiful building which for all time will be the center of our work, and especially to understand that thing which we call "the spirit of Warm Springs," which does so much to supplement the skill of science. The people of Georgia have given to this work a noble gift. In the name of the Trustees of the Foundation I thank them, and especially I thank the Georgia Hall Committee, who under the untiring efforts and leadership of Mr. Cason Callaway and Mr. Cator Woolford, have made tangible the vision of many years ago.

I am glad to be back on Georgia soil. I am hurrying to Warm Springs with special interest, for I shall see a splendid new building, given to the cause of helping crippled children by the citizens of the State of Georgia. And I am hurrying back to my cottage there for the almost equally important objective of seeing to it that a prize Georgia turkey is put into the primest possible condition for the Thanksgiving Day feast.

On this Thanksgiving, I like to think that many more fathers and mothers and children will partake of turkey than for many years past. What a splendid thing it would be if in every community throughout the land, in celebration of this Thanksgiving—and here in Georgia in celebration of the Bicentennial of the founding of the Colony—every community would set as its Thanksgiving Day objective the providing of a Thanksgiving dinner for those who have not yet been blessed by the returning prosperity sufficiently to provide their own.

Let me read to you in closing a message delivered a generation ago by a great son of a great Georgia mother, Theodore Roosevelt:

"Materially we must strive to secure a broader economic opportunity for all men so that each shall have a better chance to show the stuff of which he is made. Spirtually and ethically we must strive to bring about clean living and right thinking. We appreciate that the things of the body are important; but we appreciate also that the things of the soul are immeasurably more important. The foundation stone of national life is and ever must be the high individual character of the individual citizen."

STATEMENT ON EXTENSION OF RE-EMPLOY-MENT AGREEMENT, DECEMBER 20, 1933

The President's Re-employment Agreement according to its original terms will end on December thirty-first. At that time permanent codes of fair competition will apply to approximately 70 per cent of all employees who will eventually be covered by codes.

In the midst of winter and with many persons out of work, it is essential that the New Year should not bring with it any let down in the Recovery Program in the trades and industries which at that time have not come under approved codes and to which, therefore, only the President's Re-employment Agreement applies.

I am, therefore, inviting every employer in those trades and industries to join with me in an extension of the President's Re-employment Agreement for four months. By that time it is expected that the process of code making will have been virtually completed.

I urge all employers in trades and industries not covered by codes to co-operate by continuing to maintain higher wages and shorter hours. The need for their help is still great.

Employers joining with me in this extension of the President's Re-employment Agreement may continue to display the Blue Eagle as a symbol of their co-operation and those few employers who have not heretofore signed the agreement may sign it as extended and upon delivering a signed certificate of compliance to the Post Office may obtain a Blue Eagle.

Display of the Blue Eagle on or after Jan. 1, 1934, by an employer whose business is not entirely covered by an approved code will be treated as an acceptance of the extension of the President's Re-employment Agreement and a representation that he is complying with it for that part of his business not covered by approved codes.

ADDRESS AT THE LIGHTING OF THE COM-
MUNITY TREE IN WASHINGTON, DECEM-
BER 24, 1933

We in the Nation's capital are gathered around this symbolic tree celebrating the coming of Christmas; in spirit we join with millions of others, men and women and children, throughout our own land and in other countries and continents, in happy and reverend observance of the spirit of Christmas.

For me and for my family it is the happiest of Christmases.

To the many thousands of you who have thought of me and have sent me greetings, and I hope all of you are hearing my voice, I want to tell you how profoundly grateful I am. If it were within my power so to do I would personally thank each and every one of you for your remembrance of me, but there are so many thousands of you that that happy task is impossible.

Even more greatly, my happiness springs from the deep conviction that this year marks a greater national understanding of the significance in our modern lives of the teachings of Him whose birth we celebrate. To more and more of us the words "Thou shalt love thy neighbor as thyself" have taken on a meaning that is showing itself and proving itself in our purposes and daily lives.

May the practice of that high ideal grow in us all in the year to come.

I give you and send you one and all, old and young, a Merry Christmas and a truly Happy New Year.

And so, for now and for always "God Bless Us, Every One."

STATEMENT ON PURCHASE AND COINAGE OF SILVER, DECEMBER 31, 1933

Under the clear authority granted to me by the last session of the Congress, I have today, by proclamation, proceeded to ratify the London Agreement with regard to silver, which has already been put into effect by the Government of India, and which I understand other nations concerned are about to act on.

This proclamation, in accordance with the Act of Congress, opens our mints to the coinage of standard silver dollars from silver hereafter produced in the United States or its possessions, subject to the depositors of such silver surrendering to the Government one-half of it as seigniorage and to cover all usual charges and expenses. The dollars coined from half of such newly mined silver will be returned to the depositor. The half surrendered to the Government will be retained in the Treasury.

It will be remembered that at the London Conference 66 governments unanimously adopted the silver resolution proposed by our Government, providing in substance that these governments would refrain from the policy and practice of melting up and debasing silver coins; that they would replace low-valued paper money with silver coins; and that they would not enact legislation that would depreciate the value of silver in the world market. This resolution, however, was contingent upon an agreement between the governments of those countries producing large quantities of silver and the governments of those countries holding or using large quantities, looking to the elimination of an unnatural oversupply of silver on the markets of the world. This agreement, of course, was for the purpose of allowing demand and supply to govern the price of silver by the limitation and neutralization of this oversupply derived from the melting up of silver coins.

India had the power to dispose of, on the markets of the world, at any time, and at any price, hundreds of millions of ounces of silver. In fact, India had the power and capacity to dump silver derived from the melting up of Indian silver coins in an amount equal to the world's production from the mines—for the period of two years. This power and the uncertainty attending its execution was destructive of the value and stability of silver throughout the world.

China agreed, during the period of four years commencing Jan. 1, 1934, and ending Jan. 1, 1938, not to permit the sale of any silver derived from the debasing or melting up of silver coins. India agreed to limit the sales of such silver to a maximum of 35,000,000 ounces annually during such period and Spain agreed not to sell in excess of 5,000,000 ounces of such silver annually during such period. After such sales, these governments are to be bound by the general resolution adopted at the London Conference to which I have heretofore referred.

As a condition of the agreement by China, India and Spain, however, it was required that Australia, Canada, Mexico, Peru and the United States should take silver from the production of their respective mines to the gross amount of 35,000,000 ounces annually for such period of four years. The United States, by reason of its large population and its large silver production, agreed to take from its mines annually at least 24,421,410 ounces of silver during such period.

The production of the United States for 1932 was approximately 24,000,000 ounces of silver.

EXECUTIVE ORDER RELATING TO RECEIPT OF GOLD ON CONSIGNMENT BY THE MINTS AND ASSAY OFFICES, JANUARY 15, 1934

By virtue of the authority vested in me by section 5 (b) of the act of Oct. 6, 1917, as amended by section 2 of the act of March 9, 1933, entitled "An Act to Provide Relief in the Existing National Emergency in Banking, and for other Purposes," I, Franklin D. Roosevelt, President of the United States of America, do declare that a period of national emergency exists, and by virtue of said authority and of all other authority vested in me, do hereby prescribe the following regulations for receiving gold on consignment for sale:

Section 1. The United States mints and assay offices are hereby authorized, subject to such regulations as may from time to time be prescribed by the Secretary of the Treasury, to receive on consignment gold which the mint or assay office concerned is satisfied has not been held in noncompliance with the Executive Orders, or the orders of the Secretary of the Treasury, issued under Sections 2 and 3 of the Act of March 9, 1933, or in noncompliance with any regulations or rulings made thereunder or licenses issued pursuant thereto.

Sec. 2. The Secretary of the Treasury is hereby authorized and empowered to issue such regulations as he may deem necessary to carry out the purposes of this Executive Order.

Sec. 3. This Executive Order and any regulations issued hereunder may be modified or revoked at any time.

EXECUTIVE ORDER RELATING TO COMPLAINTS CHARGING THE PURSUIT OF MONOPOLISTIC PRACTICES, JANUARY 20, 1934

In order to effectuate the policy of Title I of the National Industrial Recovery Act, approved June 16, 1933, I, Franklin D. Roosevelt, President of the United States, pursuant to the authority thereby vested in me and in accordance with the provisions of said Act and the provisions of an Act to create a Federal Trade Commission, approved Sept. 26, 1914, do hereby direct that:

294

1. Whenever any complainant shall be dissatisfied with the disposition by any Federal agency, except the Department of Justice, of any complaint charging that any person, partnership, corporation, or other association, or form of enterprise, is engaged in any monopolistic practice, or practice permitting or promoting a monopoly, or tending to eliminate, oppress, or discriminate against small enterprises, which is allegedly in violation of the provisions of any code of fair competition approved under the National Industrial Recovery Act, or allegedly sanctioned by the provisions of such code but allegedly in violation of Section 3 (a) of said National Industrial Recovery Act, such complaint shall be transferred to the Federal Trade Commission by such agency upon request of the complainant.

2. The Federal Trade Commission may, in accordance with the provisions of the National Industrial Recovery Act and the provisions of an Act to create a Federal Trade Commission, approved Sept. 26, 1914, upon the receipt of any such complaint transmitted to it, institute a proceeding against such persons, partnerships, corporations, or other associations or form of enterprise as it may have reason to believe are engaged in the practices aforesaid, whenever it shall appear to the Federal Trade Commission that a proceeding by it in respect thereof would be to the interest of the public: *Provided*, That, if in any case the Federal Trade Commission shall determine that any such practice is not contrary to the provisions of Section 5 of the Federal Trade Commission Act or of Sections 2, 3, or 7 of the Act of Oct. 15, 1914, commonly called the Clayton Act, it shall instead of instituting such proceeding, transfer the complaint, with

the evidence and other information pertaining to the matter, to the Department of Justice.

3. The power herein conferred upon the Federal Trade Commission shall not be construed as being in derogation of any of the powers of said Commission under existing law.

STATEMENT RELATING TO FIXING OF WEIGHT OF THE GOLD DOLLAR AND THE PURCHASE OF GOLD AT A FIXED PRICE, JANUARY 31, 1934

1. Acting under the powers granted by Title 3 of the act approved May 12, 1933 (Thomas Amendment to the Farm Relief Act), the President today issued a proclamation fixing the weight of the gold dollar at 15$\frac{5}{21}$ grains nine-tenths fine. This is 59.06 plus per cent of the former weight of 25$\frac{8}{10}$ grains, nine-tenths fine, as fixed by Section 1 of the Act of Congress of March 4, 1900. The new gold content of the dollar became effective immediately on the signing of the proclamation by the President.

Under the Gold Reserve Act of 1934, signed by the President Tuesday, January thirtieth, title to the entire stock of monetary gold in the United States, including the gold coin and gold bullion heretofore held by the Federal Reserve Banks and the claim upon gold in the Treasury represented by gold certificates, is vested in the United States Government and the "profit" from the reduction of the gold content of the dollar, made effective by today's proclamation, accrues to the United States Treasury. Of this "profit" two billion dollars, under the terms of the Gold Reserve Act and of today's proclamation, constitutes a stabilization fund under the direction of the Secretary of the Treasury. The balance will be covered into the general fund of the Treasury. . . .

In his proclamation of today the President gives notice that he reserves the right, by virtue of the authority vested in him, to alter or modify the present proclamation as the interests of the United States may seem to require. The authority by later proclamations to accomplish other revaluations of the dollar in terms of gold is contained in the Gold Reserve Act signed on Tuesday.

2. The Secretary of the Treasury, with the approval of the President, issued a public announcement that beginning Feb. 1, 1934, he will buy through the Federal Reserve Bank of New York as fiscal agent, for the account of the United States, any and all gold delivered to any United States Mints or the Assay Offices in New York or Seattle, at the rate of $35.00 per fine troy ounce, less the usual Mint charges and less one-fourth of one per cent for handling charges. Purchases, however, are subject to compliance with the regulations issued under the Gold Reserve Act of 1934. . . .

REMARKS OF THE PRESIDENT TO THE BOY SCOUTS OF AMERICA, BROADCASTING A NATIONAL "CALL TO SERVICE" MOBILIZATION, FEBRUARY 10, 1934

Fellow Scouts:

I am happy to participate in the Twenty-fourth Anniversary Celebration of our organization, the Boy Scouts of America. Nearly a million of us are mobilized at this time in all parts of the country as a part of the program for this week of celebration. Home and farm patrols and troops of farm boys are joining with their brother scouts in the big cities.

In front of the City Hall in San Francisco—and it is nine o'clock in the morning there—thousands of Scouts join with other thousands in the Hippodrome in New York in carrying on the cause of world-wide brotherhood in Scouting.

As most of you know, Scouting has been one of my active interests for many years. I have visited hundreds of troops in their home towns and in their camps. I know, therefore, from personal experience the things we do and stand for as Scouts. We have ideals. We are a growing organization. We believe that we are accomplishing fine American results not only for our own membership, but also for our families, our communities and our Nation.

Summed up in one sentence, the aim of Scouting is to build up better citizenship. I believe that we are contributing greatly to that objective.

I am especially happy today to extend personal greetings and congratulations to the Scouts and Leaders who have earned the President's award for progress in the year 1933, as a part of the Ten-Year Program. It is appropriate that we are planning for the celebration of our Silver Jubilee, the Twenty-fifth Anniversary of the Boy Scouts of America, which will culminate in a great national Jamboree here in the Nation's capital in the summer of 1935. Of course it would be physically impossible for us to have the whole membership of the Boy Scouts of America, a million strong, come to Washington at one time, but I much hope that it will be possible to have every nook and cranny of our Nation represented.

As a preliminary to our Silver Jubilee, and in line with the emphasis of service for others which we have always stressed, I suggest to you that it is time once more for us to do a National Good Turn.

As many of you know, we are doing everything possible in this emergency to help suffering humanity. I called upon the Federal Emergency Relief Administrator, Mr. Harry L. Hopkins, to tell me what kind of a National Good Turn would be of the greatest service. He has recommended that during the balance of the month of February every troop and every scout do everything possible in their separate localities to collect such household furnishings, bedding and clothes, as people may be able to share as gifts to those who greatly need them.

Therefore, I ask you, under the direction of your own local officers, and in conference with the representatives of the Federal Relief Administration and other local social agencies, to gather up such of this material as may be available for distribution.

I am confident that the American people will generously co-operate and respond. Indeed, I am hoping that in many cases they will telephone or send letters to the local Scout offices to offer their help to carry through this National Good Turn.

Already I have received offers of co-operation from Governors of States, from Mayors and other community leaders. May you carry out this new Service and re-dedicate yourselves to the Scout Oath.

I ask you to join with me and the Eagle Scouts and

our President and Chief Scout Executive who are here with me in the White House in giving again the Scout Oath.

All stand!

Give the Scout sign!

Repeat with me the Scout Oath!

"On my honor I will do my best:

To do my duty to God and my country, and to obey the Scout Law;

To help other people at all times;

To keep myself physically strong, mentally awake, and morally straight."

THE

JOHN DAY

ARISE FOR IT IS DAY.

COMPANY
INC.